ASE TEST PREP A6

Electrical/Electronic Systems

THOMSON

DELMAR LEARNING

Australia Canada Mexico Singapore Spain United Kingdom United States

THOMSON

DELMAR LEARNING

Delmar's ASE Test Preparation Series
ASE Test Prep A6 Electrical/Electronic Systems

Business Unit Director:
Alar Elken

Executive Editor:
Sandy Clark

Acquisitions Editor:
San Rao

Editorial Assistant:
Bryan Viggiani

**Business and Product
Development Consultant:**
David Koontz

Developmental Editor:
Christopher Shortt

Executive Marketing Manager:
Maura Theriault

Marketing Coordinator:
Brian McGrath

Channel Manager:
Fair Huntoon

Custom Coordinator:
Claudette Corley

Executive Production Manager:
Mary Ellen Black

Production Manager:
Larry Main

Production Editor:
Tom Stover

Cover Designer:
Michael Egan

NOTICE TO THE READER

Contents

Section 1 The History of ASE

Section 2 Take and Pass Every ASE Test

Section 3 Types of Questions on an ASE Exam

Section 4 An Overview of the System

Section 5 Sample Test for Practice

Section 6 Additional Test Questions for Practice

Section 7 Appendices

Preface

This book is just one of a comprehensive series designed to prepare technicians to take and pass every ASE test. Delmar's series covers all of the Automotive tests A1 through A8 as well as Advanced Engine Performance L1 and Parts Specialist P2. The series also covers the five Collision Repair tests and the eight Medium/Heavy Duty truck tests.

Before any book in this series was written, Delmar staff met with and surveyed technicians and shop owners who have taken ASE tests and have used other preparatory materials. We found that they wanted, first and foremost, *lots* of practice tests and questions. Each book in our series contains a sample test and additional practice questions. You will be hard-pressed to find a test prep book with more questions for you to practice with. We have worked hard to ensure that these questions match the ASE style in types of questions, quantities, and level of difficulty.

Technicians also told us that they wanted to understand the ASE test and to have practical information about what they should expect. We have provided that as well, including a history of ASE and a section devoted to helping the technician "Take and Pass Every ASE Test" with case studies, test-taking strategies, and test formats.

Finally, techs wanted refresher information and references. Each of our books includes an overview section that is referenced to the task list. The complete task lists for each test appear in each book for the user's reference. There is also a complete glossary of terms for each booklet.

So whether you're looking for a sample test and a few extra questions to practice with or a complete introduction to ASE testing, with support for preparing thoroughly, this book series is an excellent answer.

We hope you benefit from this book and that you pass every ASE test you take!

Your comments, both positive and negative, are certainly encouraged! Please contact us at:

Automotive Editor
Delmar Publishers
3 Columbia Circle
Box 15015
Albany, NY 12212-5015

The History of ASE

History

Originally known as The National Institute for Automotive Service Excellence (NIASE), today's ASE was founded in 1972 as a non-profit, independent entity dedicated to improving the quality of automotive service and repair through the voluntary testing and certification of automotive technicians. Until that time, consumers had no way of distinguishing between competent and incompetent automotive mechanics. In the mid-1960s and early 1970s, efforts were made by several automotive industry affiliated associations to respond to this need. Though the associations were non-profit, many regarded certification test fees merely as a means of raising additional operating capital. Also, some associations, having a vested interest, produced test scores heavily weighted in the favor of its members.

From these efforts a new independent, non-profit association, the National Institute for Automotive Service Excellence (NIASE), was established. In early NIASE tests, Mechanic A, Mechanic B type questions were used. Over the years the trend has not changed, but in mid-1984 the term was changed to Technician A, Technician B to better emphasize sophistication of the skills needed to perform successfully in the modern motor vehicle industry. In certain tests the term used is Estimator A/B, Painter A/B, or Parts Specialist A/B. At about that same time, the logo was changed from "The Gear" to "The Blue Seal," and the organization adopted the acronym ASE for Automotive Service Excellence.

ASE

ASE's mission is to improve the quality of vehicle repair and service in the United States through the testing and certification of automotive repair technicians. Prospective candidates register for and take one or more of ASE's many exams.

Upon passing at least one exam and providing proof of two years of related work experience, the technician becomes ASE certified. A technician who passes a series of exams earns ASE Master Technician status. An automobile technician, for example, must pass eight exams for this recognition.

The exams, conducted twice a year at over seven hundred locations around the country, are administered by American College Testing (ACT). They stress real-world diagnostic and repair problems. Though a good knowledge of theory is helpful to the technician in answering many of the questions, there are no questions specifically on theory. Certification is valid for five years. To retain certification, the technician must be retested to renew his or her certificate.

The automotive consumer benefits because ASE certification is a valuable yardstick by which to measure the knowledge and skills of individual technicians, as well as their commitment to their chosen profession. It is also a tribute to the repair facility employing ASE certified technicians. ASE certified technicians are permitted to wear blue and white ASE shoulder insignia, referred to as the "Blue Seal of Excellence," and carry credentials listing their areas of expertise. Often employers display their technicians' credentials in the customer waiting area. Customers look for facilities that display ASE's Blue Seal of Excellence logo on outdoor signs, in the customer waiting area, in the telephone book (Yellow Pages), and in newspaper advertisements.

To become ASE certified, contact:

National Institute for Automotive Service Excellence
13505 Dulles Technology Drive
Herndon, VA 20171-3421

2 Take and Pass Every ASE Test

ASE Testing

Participating in an Automotive Service Excellence (ASE) voluntary certification program gives you a chance to show your customers that you have the "know-how" needed to work on today's modern vehicles. The ASE certification tests allow you to compare your skills and knowledge to the automotive service industry's standards for each specialty area.

If you are the "average" automotive technician taking this test, you are in your mid-thirties and have not attended school for about fifteen years. That means you probably have not taken a test in many years. Some of you, on the other hand, have attended college or taken postsecondary education courses and may be more familiar with taking tests and with test-taking strategies. There is, however, a difference in the ASE test you are preparing to take and the educational tests you may be accustomed to.

Who Writes the Questions?

The questions on all ASE tests are written by service industry experts familiar with all aspects of the subject area. ASE questions are entirely job-related and designed to test the skills that you need to know on the job.

The questions originate in an ASE "item-writing" workshop where service representatives from domestic and import automobile manufacturers, parts and equipment manufacturers, and vocational educators meet in a workshop setting to share their ideas and translate them into test questions. Each test question written by these experts is reviewed by all of the members of the group.

All of the questions are pretested and quality-checked in a nonscoring section of tests by a national sample of certifying technicians. The questions that meet ASE's high standards of accuracy and quality are then included in the scoring sections of future tests. Those questions that do not pass ASE's stringent test are sent back to the workshop or are discarded. ASE's tests are monitored by an independent proctor and are administered and machine-scored by an independent provider, American College Testing (ACT).

Objective Tests

A test is called an objective test if the same standards and conditions apply to everyone taking the test and there is only one correct answer to each question. Objective tests primarily measure your ability to recall information. A well-designed objective test can also test your ability to understand, analyze, interpret, and apply your knowledge. Objective tests include true-false, multiple choice, fill in the blank, and matching questions. ASE's tests consist exclusively of four-part multiple-choice objective questions.

Before beginning to take an objective test, quickly look over the test to determine the number of questions, but do not try to read through all of the questions. In an ASE test, there are usually between forty and eighty questions, depending on the subject. Read through each question before marking your answer. Answer the questions in the order they appear on the test. Leave the questions blank that you are not sure of and move on to the next question. You can return to those unanswered questions after you have finished the others. They may be easier to answer at a later time after your mind has had additional time to consider them on a subconscious level. In addition, you might find information in other questions that will help you to answer some of them.

Do not be obsessed by the apparent pattern of responses. For example, do not be influenced by a pattern like **d, c, b, a, d, c, b, a** on an ASE test.

There is also a lot of folk wisdom about taking objective tests. For example, there are those who would advise you to avoid response options that use certain words such as *all, none, always, never, must,* and *only,* to name a few. This, they claim, is because nothing in life is exclusive. They would advise you to choose response options that use words that allow for some exception, such as *sometimes, frequently, rarely, often, usually, seldom,* and *normally.* They would also advise you to avoid the first and last option (A and D) because test writers, they feel, are more comfortable if they put the correct answer in the middle (B and C) of the choices. Another recommendation often offered is to select the option that is either shorter or longer than the other three choices because it is more likely to be correct. Some would advise you to never change an answer since your first intuition is usually correct.

Although there may be a grain of truth in this folk wisdom, ASE test writers try to avoid them and so should you. There are just as many **A** answers as there are **B** answers, just as many **D** answers as **C** answers. As a matter of fact, ASE tries to balance the answers at about 25 percent per choice **A, B, C,** and **D.** There is no intention to use "tricky" words, such as outlined above. Put no credence in the opposing words "sometimes" and "never," for example.

Multiple-choice tests are sometimes challenging because there are often several choices that may seem possible, and it may be difficult to decide on the correct choice. The best strategy, in this case, is to first determine the correct answer before looking at the options. If you see the answer you decided on, you should still examine the options to make sure that none seem more correct than yours. If you do not know or are not sure of the answer, read each option very carefully and try to eliminate those options that you know to be wrong. That way, you can often arrive at the correct choice through a process of elimination.

If you have gone through all of the test and you still do not know the answer to some of the questions, then guess. Yes, guess. You then have at least a 25 percent chance of being correct. If you leave the question blank, you have no chance. In ASE tests, there is no penalty for being wrong.

Preparing for the Exam

The main reason we have included so many sample and practice questions in this guide is, simply, to help you learn what you know and what you don't know. We recommend that you work your way through each question in this book. Before doing this, carefully look through Section 3; it contains a description and explanation of the questions you'll find in an ASE exam.

Once you know what the questions will look like, move to the sample test. After you have answered one of the sample questions (Section 5), read the explanation (Section 7) to the answer for that question. If you don't feel you understand the reasoning for the correct answer, go back and read the overview (Section 4) for the task that is related to that question. If you still don't feel you have a solid understanding of the material, identify a good source of information on the topic, such as a textbook, and do some more studying.

After you have completed the sample test, move to the additional questions (Section 6). This time answer the questions as if you were taking an actual test. Once you have answered all of the questions, grade your results using the answer key in Section 7. For every question that you gave a wrong answer to, study the explanations to the answers and/or the overview of the related task areas.

Here are some basic guidelines to follow while preparing for the exam:

- Focus your studies on those areas you are weak in.
- Be honest with yourself while determining if you understand something.
- Study often but in short periods of time.
- Remove yourself from all distractions while studying.
- Keep in mind the goal of studying is not just to pass the exam, the real goal is to learn!

During the Test

Mark your bubble sheet clearly and accurately. One of the biggest problems an adult faces in test-taking, it seems, is in placing an answer in the correct spot on a bubble sheet. Make certain that you mark your answer for, say, question 21, in the space on the bubble sheet designated for the answer for question 21. A correct response in the wrong bubble will probably be wrong. Remember, the answer sheet is machine scored and can only "read" what you have bubbled in. Also, do not bubble in two answers for the same question.

If you finish answering all of the questions on a test ahead of time, go back and review the answers of those questions that you were not sure of. You can often catch careless errors by using the remaining time to review your answers.

At practically every test, some technicians will invariably finish ahead of time and turn their papers in long before the final call. Do not let them distract or intimidate you. Either they knew too little and could not finish the test, or they were very self-confident and thought they knew it all. Perhaps they were trying to impress the proctor or other technicians about how much they know. Often you may hear them later talking about the information they knew all the while but forgot to respond on their answer sheet.

It is not wise to use less than the total amount of time that you are allotted for a test. If there are any doubts, take the time for review. Any product can usually be made better with some additional effort. A test is no exception. It is not necessary to turn in your test paper until you are told to do so.

Your Test Results!

You can gain a better perspective about tests if you know and understand how they are scored. ASE's tests are scored by American College Testing (ACT), a non-partial, non-biased organization having no vested interest in ASE or in the automotive industry. Each question carries the same weight as any other question. For example, if there are fifty questions, each is worth 2 percent of the total score. The passing grade is 70 percent. That means you must correctly answer thirty-five of the fifty questions to pass the test.

The test results can tell you:
- where your knowledge equals or exceeds that needed for competent performance, or
- where you might need more preparation.

The test results *cannot* tell you:
- how you compare with other technicians, or
- how many questions you answered correctly.

Your ASE test score report will show the number of correct answers you got in each of the content areas. These numbers provide information about your performance in each area of the test. However, because there may be a different number of questions in each area of the test, a high percentage of correct answers in an area with few questions may not offset a low percentage in an area with many questions.

It may be noted that one does not "fail" an ASE test. The technician who does not pass is simply told "More Preparation Needed." Though large differences in percentages may indicate problem areas, it is important to consider how many questions were asked in each area. Since each test evaluates all phases of the work involved in a service specialty, you should be prepared in each area. A low score in one area could keep you from passing an entire test.

There is no such thing as average. You cannot determine your overall test score by adding the percentages given for each task area and dividing by the number of areas. It doesn't work that way because there generally are not the same number of questions in each task area. A task area with twenty questions, for example, counts more toward your total score than a task area with ten questions.

Your test report should give you a good picture of your results and a better understanding of your task areas of strength and weakness.

If you fail to pass the test, you may take it again at any time it is scheduled to be administered. You are the only one who will receive your test score. Test scores will not be given over the telephone by ASE nor will they be released to anyone without your written permission.

3 Types of Questions on an ASE Exam

ASE certification tests are often thought of as being tricky. They may seem to be tricky if you do not completely understand what is being asked. The following examples will help you recognize certain types of ASE questions and avoid common errors.

Each test is made up of forty to eighty multiple-choice questions. Multiple-choice questions are an efficient way to test knowledge. To answer them correctly, you must think about each choice as a possibility, and then choose the one that best answers the question. To do this, read each word of the question carefully. Do not assume you know what the question is about until you have finished reading it.

About 10 percent of the questions on an actual ASE exam will use an illustration. These drawings contain the information needed to correctly answer the question. The illustration must be studied carefully before attempting to answer the question. Often, techs look at the possible answers then try to match up the answers with the drawing. Always do the opposite; match the drawing to the answers. When the illustration is showing an electrical schematic or another system in detail, look over the system and try to figure out how the system works before you look at the question and the possible answers.

Multiple-Choice Questions

One type of multiple-choice question has three wrong answers and one correct answer. The wrong answers, however, may be almost correct, so be careful not to jump at the first answer that seems to be correct. If all the answers seem to be correct, choose the answer that is the most correct. If you readily know the answer, this kind of question does not present a problem. If you are unsure of the answer, analyze the question and the answers. For example:

A rocker panel is a structural member of which vehicle construction type?

A. Front-wheel drive
B. Pickup truck
C. Unibody
D. Full-frame

Analysis:

This question asks for a specific answer. By carefully reading the question, you will find that it asks for a construction type that uses the rocker panel as a structural part of the vehicle.

Answer A is wrong. Front-wheel drive is not a vehicle construction type.

Answer B is wrong. A pickup truck is not a type of vehicle construction.

Answer C is correct. Unibody design creates structural integrity by welding parts together, such as the rocker panels, but does not require exterior cosmetic panels installed for full strength.

Answer D is wrong. Full-frame describes a body-over-frame construction type that relies on the frame assembly for structural integrity.

Therefore, the correct answer is C. If the question was read quickly and the words "construction type" were passed over, answer A may have been selected.

EXCEPT Questions

Another type of question used on ASE tests has answers that are all correct except one. The correct answer for this type of question is the answer that is wrong. The word "EXCEPT" will always be in capital letters. You must identify which of the choices is the wrong answer. If you read quickly through the question, you may overlook what the question is asking and answer the question with the first correct statement. This will make your answer wrong. An example of this type of question and the analysis is as follows:

All of the following are tools for the analysis of structural damage EXCEPT:

A. height gauge.
B. tape measure.
C. dial indicator.
D. tram gauge.

Analysis:

The question really requires you to identify the tool that is not used for analyzing structural damage. All tools given in the choices are used for analyzing structural damage except one. This question presents two basic problems for the test-taker who reads through the question too quickly. It may be possible to read over the word "EXCEPT" in the question or not think about which type of damage analysis would use answer C. In either case, the correct answer may not be selected. To correctly answer this question, you should know what tools are used for the analysis of structural damage. If you cannot immediately recognize the incorrect tool, you should be able to identify it by analyzing the other choices.

Answer A is wrong. A height gauge *may* be used to analyze structural damage.

Answer B is wrong. A tape measure may be used to analyze structural damage.

Answer C is correct. A dial indicator may be used as a damage analysis tool for moving parts, such as wheels, wheel hubs, and axle shafts, but would not be used to measure structural damage.

Answer D is wrong. A tram gauge *is* used to measure structural damage.

Technician A, Technician B Questions

The type of question that is most popularly associated with an ASE test is the "Technician A says. . . Technician B says. . . Who is right?" type. In this type of question, you must identify the correct statement or statements. To answer this type of question correctly, you must carefully read each technician's statement and judge it on its own merit to determine if the statement is true.

Typically, this type of question begins with a statement about some analysis or repair procedure. This is followed by two statements about the cause of the problem, proper inspection, identification, or repair choices. You are asked whether the first statement, the second statement, both statements, or neither statement is correct. Analyzing this type of question is a little easier than the other types because there are only two ideas to consider although there are still four choices for an answer.

Technician A, Technician B questions are really double true or false questions. The best way to analyze this kind of question is to consider each technician's statement separately. Ask yourself, is A true or false? Is B true or false? Then select your answer from the four choices. An important point to remember is that an ASE Technician A, Technician B question will never have Technician A and B directly disagreeing with each other. That is why you must evaluate each statement independently. An example of this type of question and the analysis of it follows.

Structural dimensions are being measured. Technician A says comparing measurements from one side to the other is enough to determine the damage. Technician

B says a tram gauge can be used when a tape measure cannot measure in a straight line from point to point. Who is right?

A. A only

B. B only

C. Both A and B

D. Neither A nor B

Analysis:

With some vehicles built asymmetrically, side-to-side measurements are not always equal. The manufacturer's specifications need to be verified with a dimension chart before reaching any conclusions about the structural damage.

Answer A is wrong. Technician A's statement is wrong. A tram gauge would provide a point-to-point measurement when a part, such as a strut tower or air cleaner, interrupts a direct line between the points.

Answer B is correct. Technician B is correct. A tram gauge can be used when a tape measure cannot be used to measure in a straight line from point to point.

Answer C is wrong. Since Technician A is not correct, C cannot be the correct answer.

Answer D is wrong. Since Technician B is correct, D cannot be the correct answer.

Most-Likely Questions

Most-likely questions are somewhat difficult because only one choice is correct while the other three choices are nearly correct. An example of a most-likely-cause question is as follows:

The most likely cause of reduced turbocharger boost pressure may be a:

A. westgate valve stuck closed.

B. westgate valve stuck open.

C. leaking westgate diaphragm.

D. disconnected westgate linkage.

Analysis:

Answer A is wrong. A westgate valve stuck closed increases turbocharger boost pressure.

Answer B is correct. A westgate valve stuck open decreases turbocharger boost pressure.

Answer C is wrong. A leaking westgate valve diaphragm increases turbocharger boost pressure.

Answer D is wrong. A disconnected westgate valve linkage will increase turbocharger boost pressure.

LEAST-Likely Questions

Notice that in most-likely questions there is no capitalization. This is not so with LEAST-likely type questions. For this type of question, look for the choice that would be the least likely cause of the described situation. Read the entire question carefully before choosing your answer. An example is as follows:

What is the LEAST likely cause of a bent pushrod?

A. Excessive engine speed

B. A sticking valve

C. Excessive valve guide clearance

D. A worn rocker arm stud

Analysis:

Answer A is wrong. Excessive engine speed may cause a bent pushrod.

Answer B is wrong. A sticking valve may cause a bent pushrod.

Answer C is correct. Excessive valve clearance will not generally cause a bent pushrod.

Answer D is wrong. A worn rocker arm stud may cause a bent pushrod.

Summary

There are no four-part multiple-choice ASE questions having "none of the above" or "all of the above" choices. ASE does not use other types of questions, such as fill-in-the-blank, completion, true-false, word-matching, or essay. ASE does not require you to draw diagrams or sketches. If a formula or chart is required to answer a question, it is provided for you. There are no ASE questions that require you to use a pocket calculator.

Testing Time Length

An ASE test session is four hours and fifteen minutes. You may attempt from one to a maximum of four tests in one session. It is recommended, however, that no more than a total of 225 questions be attempted at any test session. This will allow for just over one minute for each question.

Visitors are not permitted at any time. If you wish to leave the test room, for any reason, you must first ask permission. If you finish your test early and wish to leave, you are permitted to do so only during specified dismissal periods.

You should monitor your progress and set an arbitrary limit to how much time you will need for each question. This should be based on the number of questions you are attempting. It is suggested that you wear a watch because some facilities may not have a clock visible to all areas of the room.

4 An Overview of the System

Electrical/Electronic Systems (Test A6)

The following section includes the task areas and task lists for this test and a written overview of the topics covered in the test.

The task list describes the actual work you should be able to do as a technician that you will be tested on by the ASE. This is your key to the test and you should review this section carefully. We have based our sample test and additional questions upon these tasks, and the overview section will also support your understanding of the task list. ASE advises that the questions on the test may not equal the number of tasks listed; the task lists tell you what ASE expects you to know how to do and be ready to be tested upon.

At the end of each question in the Sample Test and Additional Test Questions sections, a letter and number will be used as a reference back to this section for additional study. Note the following example: **D.7.**

Task List

D. Charging System Diagnosis and Repair (6 Questions)

Task D.7   Inspect, repair, or replace connectors and wires of charging circuits.

Example:

30. All of these statements about wiring service are true EXCEPT:
    A. acid core solder must be used for electrical soldering.
    B. rosin core solder must be used for electrical soldering.
    C. if a broken wire contains a drain wire, join this wire separately.
    D. heat a crimp and seal sleeve until sealant appears at each end of the sleeve.

(D.7)

Analysis:

Question #30
Answer A is correct.
Answer B is wrong. Rosin core solder must be used for electrical soldering.
Answer C is wrong. Drain wire should be soldered separately.
Answer D is wrong. Crimp and seal sleeves should be heated until sealant appears at both ends.

Task List and Overview

A. General Electrical/Electronic System Diagnosis (13 Questions)

Task A.1

Check electrical circuits with a test light; determine needed repairs.

Continuity in an electric circuit may be tested with a 12V test lamp. Connect the test light lead to ground. With voltage supplied to the circuit, begin at the battery and connect the test light to various terminals in the circuit. When the test light is not illuminated, the open circuit is between the terminal where the test light is connected and the last terminal where the test light was illuminated.

Task A.2

Check voltages and voltage drops in electrical/electronic circuits with a voltmeter; interpret readings and determine needed repairs.

A voltmeter may be connected across a component in a circuit to measure the voltage drop across the component. Current must be flowing through the circuit during the voltage drop test. The amount of voltage drop depends on the resistance in the component and the amount of current flow.

Task A.3

Check current flow in electrical/electronic circuits and components with an ammeter; interpret readings and determine needed repairs.

An ammeter has low internal resistance, and the meter must be connected in series with a circuit. Some ammeters have an inductive clamp that fits over a wire in the circuit. These ammeters measure the current flow from the strength of the magnetic field surrounding the wire. High current flow is caused by high voltage or low resistance. Conversely, low current flow results from high resistance or low voltage.

Task A.4

Check continuity and resistances in electrical/electronic circuits and components with an ohmmeter; interpret readings and determine needed repairs.

An ohmmeter has an internal power source. Meter damage may result if it is connected to a live circuit. Most currently produced ohmmeters are auto-ranging (automatically selecting the proper resistance range), if not, be sure to select the proper range when measuring a circuit. For example, when a component has resistance of 10,000 ohms, select the X1000 range.

Because of the internal power source, an ohmmeter should not be used when testing SIR components with pyrotechnic components.

Task A.5

Check electronic circuit waveforms using an oscilloscope; interpret readings and determine needed repairs.

An oscilloscope converts electrical signals into a visual image representing voltage changes over a specific period of time. An upward movement of the trace means the voltage has increased, whereas a downward movement means the voltage has decreased. If the trace stays flat, the voltage is staying at that level. As the trace moves across the screen of the oscilloscope, time is represented.

The size and clarity of the trace is dependent on the voltage scale and the time reference selected by the technician. Most scopes are equipped with control, that allow voltage and time interval selection.

Analog scopes show the actual activity of a circuit and are referred to as "real-time" scopes. Digital scopes convert the voltage signals into digital signals; therefore, some delay between the electrical activity and the display is experienced. This delay does give the trace a cleaner appearance as an analog trace is only clean when the voltage has been constant for some time.

Observation of the electrical activity of a component is one of the best ways to diagnose an electronic circuit. Abnormal traces and abnormal trace changes in response to operating conditions are great indicators for further diagnosis and/or for identification of faulty components or circuits.

Task A.6

Use scan tool data to diagnose electronic systems; interpret readings and determine needed repairs.

A scan tool is a microprocessor designed to communicate with the vehicle's computer. Connected to the computer through a diagnostic connector, a scan tool can access trouble codes, run tests to check system operations, and monitor the activity of a system.

The data displayed on a scan tool should be compared to the expected or known good data tables given in the service manual for the vehicle being tested. Depending on the year of the vehicle and the system it is equipped with, the trouble codes displayed on the scan tool may indicate a general problem area or may identify a specific part of a circuit. Observing the activity of various inputs and outputs can lead a technician to problems that may be related or unrelated to the computer system.

Task A.7

Check electrical/electronic circuits with jumper wires; determine needed repairs.

A fused jumper wire may be used to bypass a part of a circuit to locate a defect in the circuit. When a component is bypassed with a jumper wire and the circuit operation is restored to normal, the bypassed component is defective.

Task A.8

Find shorts, grounds, opens, and resistance problems in electrical/electronic circuits; determine needed repairs.

A high resistance problem may be diagnosed by measuring the voltage drop across various system components. High resistance in a component causes higher than specified voltage drop. A short to the ground may be diagnosed by connecting a 12V test light in place of the circuit fuse. With the circuit switch on, disconnect connectors beginning at the load. When the 12V test light remains on, the short to the ground is between the test light and the disconnected connector. If the test light goes out, the short to the ground is between the disconnected connector and the load.

Task A.9

Measure and diagnose the cause(s) of abnormal key-off battery drain (parasitic draw); determine needed repairs.

Many car manufacturers recommend measuring battery drain with a tester switch connected in series at the negative battery terminal. The drain test procedure must be followed in the vehicle manufacturer's service manual. A multimeter with a milliampere scale is connected in parallel to the tester switch. When the tester switch is open, any current drain from the battery must flow through the tester switch. Some computers require several minutes after the ignition switch is turned off before they enter sleep mode with a reduced current drain. Therefore, after the ignition switch is turned off and the tester switch is opened, wait for the specified time before recording the milliampere reading. Some vehicle manufacturers specify a maximum battery drain of 50 milliamperes. Other vehicle manufacturers specify the battery drain is calculated by dividing the battery reserve capacity rating by four.

Task A.10

Inspect, test, and replace fusible links, circuit breakers, fuses, and other current limiting devices.

When an ohmmeter is connected to a circuit breaker, fuse, or fuse link, the meter should read zero ohms if the component is working properly. An open circuit breaker, fuse, or fuse link causes an infinite ohmmeter reading. The current flow from an ohmmeter does not cause an automotive circuit breaker to open. A diode can be checked with an analog DVOM. Resistance should be high when the meter is connected across the diode and low when the leads are reversed.

Task A.11

Read and interpret electrical schematic diagrams and symbols.

All components have a special shape so they can be identified around the world on schematics. Some common components are shown in the figure.

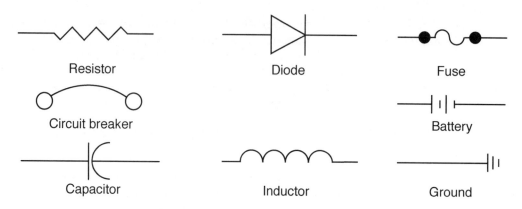

Resistor	Diode	Fuse
Circuit breaker		Battery
Capacitor	Inductor	Ground

B. Battery Diagnosis and Service (4 Questions)

Task B.1

Perform battery state of charge test; determine needed service.

When performing a battery state of charge test with a hydrometer, you should subtract 0.004 specific gravity points from the hydrometer reading for every 10°F (5.6°C) of electrolyte temperature below 80°F (26.7°C). During this test, 0.004 specific gravity points must be added to the hydrometer reading for every 10°F (5.6°C) of electrolyte temperature above 80°F (26.7°C). The maximum variation is 0.050 in cell-specific gravity readings. When all the cell readings exceed 1.265, the battery is fully charged.

Task B.2

Perform battery capacity (load, high rate discharge) test; determine needed service.

The battery discharge rate for a capacity test is usually one-half of the cold cranking rating. The battery is discharged at the proper rate for 15 seconds, and the battery voltage must remain above 9.6V with the battery temperature at 70°F (21.1°C) or above. The lower the temperature, the lower the voltage.

Task B.3

Maintain or restore electronic memory functions.

If battery voltage is disconnected from a computer, the adaptive memory in the computer is erased. In the case of a powertrain control module (PCM), disconnecting the power may cause erratic engine operation or erratic transmission shifting when the engine is restarted. After the vehicle is driven for about 20 miles (32 kilometers), the computer relearns the system, and normal operation is restored. If the vehicle is equipped with personalized items, such as memory seats or mirrors, the memory will be erased in the computer that controls these items. Radio station presets will also be erased. A 12V power supply from a dry cell battery may be connected through the cigarette lighter or power point connector to maintain voltage to the electrical system when the battery is disconnected.

Task B.4
Inspect, clean, fill, or replace battery.

A battery may be cleaned with a baking soda and water solution. Cleaning the battery will eliminate surface discharge across the top of the battery. The electrolyte level should be checked and adjusted in batteries with removable caps. Maintenance-free batteries with built-in hydrometers indicate a low electrolyte level when the hydrometer is light yellow or clear. If electrolyte is low, the battery should be replaced. A low electrolyte level can be caused by a faulty voltage regulator that causes overcharging. When disconnecting battery cables, always disconnect the negative cable first.

Task B.5
Perform slow/fast battery charge in accordance with manufacturer's recommendations.

If the battery is charged in the vehicle, the battery cables should be disconnected during the charging procedure. The charging time depends on the battery state of charge and the battery capacity. If the battery temperature exceeds 125°F (51.7°C) while charging, the battery may be damaged. When fast charging a battery, reduce the charging rate when specific gravity reaches 1.225 to avoid excessive battery gassing. The battery is fully charged when the specific gravity increases to 1.265. Do not attempt to fast charge a cold battery.

Task B.6
Inspect, clean, and repair or replace battery cables, connectors, clamps, and holddowns.

When removing battery clamps, care should be taken not to stress the battery terminals. The clamps should be loosened first and then removed. If they do not come off readily, a commercially available puller should be used. Do not pry or apply sideways force to the terminals in order to avoid battery damage. Terminal contact surfaces should be cleaned with a suitable tool until the surfaces are clean and bright, thus assuring good contact.

It is always wise to spray the cable clamps with a protective coating to prevent corrosion. Grease or petroleum jelly will also help prevent corrosion. Protective pads are available that go under the clamp and around the terminal to inhibit corrosion.

Task B.7
Jump-start a vehicle with jumper cables and a booster battery or auxiliary power supply.

The accessories must be off in both vehicles during the boost procedure. The negative booster cable must be connected to an engine ground in the vehicle being boosted. Always connect the positive booster cable followed by the negative booster cable, and complete the negative cable connection last on the vehicle being boosted. Do not allow vehicles to contact each other. When disconnecting the booster cables, remove the negative booster cable first on the vehicle being boosted.

C. Starting System Diagnosis and Repair (5 Questions)

Task C.1
Perform starter current draw test; determine needed repairs.

Perform a starter draw test using a suitable instrument (VAT-40, etc.). Follow the manufacturer's direction for measuring starter draw. Observe current flow, cranking speed, and voltage, in order to determine starter system condition.

High starter current draw, low cranking speed, and low cranking voltage usually indicates a defective starter. This condition may also be caused by internal engine problems, such as partially seized bearings. Low current draw, low cranking speed, and high cranking voltage indicates excessive resistance in the starter circuit.

Task C.2

Perform starter circuit voltage drop tests; determine needed repairs.

Measure the voltage drop across each component in the starter circuit to check the resistance in that part of the circuit. The ignition and fuel system must be disabled while making these tests. Read the voltage drop across each component while the starting motor is operating. For example, connect the voltmeter leads to the positive battery terminal and the positive cable on the starter solenoid, and crank the engine to measure the voltage drop across the positive battery cable.

Task C.3

Inspect, test, and repair or replace switches, connectors, and wires of starter control circuits.

Relays and switches in the starting motor circuit may be tested with an ohmmeter. When an ohmmeter is connected across the relay or switch contacts, the meter should provide an infinite reading if the contacts are open. If the relay or switch contacts are closed, the ohmmeter reading should be at, or near, zero. When the ohmmeter leads are connected across the terminals that are connected to the relay winding, the meter should indicate the specified resistance. A resistance below the specified value indicates a shorted winding, whereas an infinite reading proves that the winding is open.

Task C.4

Inspect, test, and replace starter relays and solenoids.

The ohmmeter leads must be connected across the solenoid terminal and the field coil terminal to test the pull-in winding. Connect the ohmmeter leads from the solenoid terminal to the ground to test the hold-in winding.

Task C.5

Remove and replace starter.

When reinstalling the starter motor, perform a free spin test or a current draw test. Also test the pinion gear clearance. This is done by disconnecting the M terminal so the pinion gear will shift into the cranking position. Then check the clearance with a feeler gauge. Normally, specifications call for a clearance of 0.010 to 0.040 in (0.25 to 1.01 mm).

Task C.6

Differentiate between electrical and engine mechanical problems that cause a slow crank or no crank condition.

The first step to checking a starting problem should be to check the battery condition. Many starting problems are actually contributable to battery problems. Do a complete series of battery tests to confirm the condition of the battery. Perform a visual inspection of the starter system to find loose connectors and frayed wires. After the visual inspection, if the engine will not turn over, try to turn the engine over by using a large socket wrench to turn the crankshaft pulley nut. If the engine cannot be rotated, then the engine may be seized.

D. Charging System Diagnosis and Repair (5 Questions)

(Note: In 1996 SAE J1930 terminology was adapted to standardized component identification. This standard adopted the name "generator" to refer to the component commonly known as an "alternator." Both terms are used interchangeably in the ASE tests.)

Task D.1

Diagnose charging system problems that cause an undercharge, a no-charge, or an overcharge condition.

A low charging voltage caused by a defective voltage regulator or alternator results in a reduced charging rate and an undercharged battery. This problem also may be caused by a loose alternator belt or excessive resistance in the wire from the alternator battery terminal to the positive battery terminal. An overcharged battery is usually caused by a defective voltage regulator that allows high charging circuit voltage. A no-charge condition may be caused by an open alternator field circuit or an open fuse link in the wire leading from the alternator battery terminal to the positive battery terminal.

Task D.2

Inspect, adjust, and replace generator (alternator) drive belts, pulleys, and tensioners.

An undercharged battery may be caused by a slipping alternator belt. A slipping belt may be caused by insufficient belt tension or a worn, glazed, or oil-soaked belt. Belt tension may be tested with a belt tension gauge or by measuring the belt deflection in the center of the belt span. A belt should have 0.5 in (12.7 mm) of deflection for every foot (30.5 cm) of free span. Many serpentine belts have an automatic spring loaded tensioner with a belt wear scale.

Task D.3

Perform charging system output test; determine needed repairs.

The alternator belt tension and condition should be checked before an output test is performed. Turn off the vehicle accessories during the test. If the alternator is full-fielded during the output test, a carbon pile load in the volt ampere tester must be used to maintain the voltage below 15V. The alternator output may be tested by lowering the voltage to the voltage specified by the vehicle manufacturer.

Task D.4

Perform generator (alternator) output test; determine needed repairs.

Use a commercially available charging system tester (VAT-40, etc.), to determine generator (alternator) output.

When the output is zero during the test, the field circuit is probably open. This problem is usually caused by worn brushes or an open field winding in the rotor. If output is less than specified, there is probably a problem with the diodes or stator. A high resistance in the field winding also reduces output. When the alternator is full-fielded to test output, the voltage regulator is bypassed and does not affect output. Never full-field an alternator longer than 30 seconds.

Task D.5

Inspect, test, or replace voltage regulator/regulating circuit; determine needed repairs.

When the alternator voltage is erratic or too low, the alternator may be full-fielded to determine the cause of the problem. When the alternator is full-fielded and the alternator current and voltage output are normal, the voltage regulator is probably defective. If the charging system voltage is higher than specified, the voltage regulator is probably defective. On a charging system with an external regulator, this problem may be caused by excessive resistance in the field circuit between the ignition switch and the regulator. Overcharging ruins batteries.

Task D.6

Perform charging circuit voltage drop test; determine needed repairs.

A voltmeter may be connected from the alternator battery wire to the positive battery terminal to measure voltage drop in the charging circuit. Many car manufacturers recommend a 10 ampere charging rate while measuring this voltage drop. When the voltage drop is more than specified, the circuit resistance is excessive. High charging circuit resistance between the alternator battery terminal and the positive battery terminal may cause an undercharged battery.

Task D.7

Inspect, repair, or replace connectors and wires of charging circuits.

Rosin core solder should always be used when repairing electrical circuits by soldering. Always insulate bare wires with heat shrink tubing or high quality electrical tape, properly applied. If the wire contains a shield wire, solder the drain wire separately. When using a heat and crimp seal, apply heat until the sealant appears at both ends. Butt (swage) connectors are suitable if care is taken to strip the proper amount of insulation from the wires. This will ensure adequate engagement in the connector without exposing the bare conductor. These connectors are not suitable in corrosion prone areas.

Task D.8

Remove, inspect, and replace generator (alternator).

Disconnect the negative battery terminal before removing the alternator. If the vehicle is equipped with an air bag system, wait for the time specified by the vehicle manufacturer, and then begin the alternator removal procedure.

E. Lighting Systems Diagnosis and Repair (6 Questions)
1. Headlights, Parking Lights, Taillights, Dash Lights, and Courtesy Lights (3 Questions)

Task E.1.1

Diagnose the cause of brighter than normal, intermittent, dim, or no operation of headlights.

If the headlights are inoperative, check the circuit breakers or fuses. Many headlight circuits have a circuit breaker in the headlight switch. If the headlights are dim, check for resistance in the headlight circuit. If headlights become brighter when the engine is accelerated, high charge system voltage is probably the cause. When the headlight operation is intermittent, check for an intermittent open or short circuit in the headlight wiring, dimmer switch, or headlight switch. Intermittent headlight operation also may be caused by a shorted condition or a short to ground. Either of these conditions causes excessive current flow in the circuit that may cause the circuit breaker to open. This action turns off the headlights. When the circuit breaker cools, the headlights come back on.

Task E.1.2

Inspect, test, and repair daytime running light systems.

Daytime running lights (DRL) are typically part of the vehicle's high-beam circuit. The control circuit is connected directly to the vehicle's ignition switch so the lights are turned on whenever the vehicle is running. The circuit is equipped with a module that reduces battery voltage to approximately 6- volts. This voltage reduction allows the high beams to burn with less intensity and prolongs the life of the bulbs. When the headlight switch is moved to the ON position, the module is deactivated and the lights work normally.

Diagnosis of these systems should begin identifying whether the problem is in the DRL system or the headlight system. If the problem is in the headlight system, service to the circuit and lamps is conducted in the same way as for vehicles that are not equipped with DRL. If the problem is in the DRL system and the headlights work normally, only that part of the circuit that is unique to the DRL can be the problem.

Task E.1.3

Inspect, replace, and aim headlights/bulbs and auxiliary lights (fog lights/driving lights).

Always turn off the lights and allow the bulbs to cool before changing halogen bulbs. Keep moisture away from the bulb, and handle the bulb only by its base. Do not scratch or drop the bulb. Coat the terminals of the bulb or at the connector with dielectric grease to minimize corrosion. Sealed beam and standard bulbs should be placed securely into their retaining plates or fixtures.

Task E.1.4

Inspect, test, and repair or replace headlight and dimmer switches, relays, control units, sensors, sockets, connectors, and wires of headlight circuits.

Some headlight switches have a button on the case that is designed to release the headlight knob. Some switches contain a circuit breaker that is connected to the headlamp system. Other lighting systems will have separate fuses. The dimmer switch is connected in series between the switch and the headlamps. When the current is turned on, the dimmer switch directs the current flow to the selected bulb.

Task E.1.5

Diagnose the cause of intermittent, slow, or no operation of retractable headlight assembly.

Some headlamp door retractors are vacuum operated. Any engine condition that would cause low vacuum will slow or prevent headlamp door operation. The vacuum system is generally used to close the headlamp door.

Electrically operated systems generally incorporate a headlamp control module which provides power to the headlamp door motors in response to signals received from the headlamp circuit.

Task E.1.6

Inspect, test, and repair or replace motors, switches, relays, connectors, wires, and controllers of retractable headlight assembly circuits.

When the driver turns the headlights on, voltage is supplied from the battery through the headlight switch to Terminal A on the headlight door module. In response to this signal, the headlight door module supplies voltage to both headlight door motors. This action operates both motors to open the headlight doors. If the headlights are shut off, the module reverses the motor action to close the doors. Some headlight door motors have a manual knob on the headlight door motors. If the motors do not open the doors, this knob may be rotated to lift the doors.

Task E.1.7

Diagnose the cause of brighter than normal, intermittent, dim, or no operation of parking lights, taillights, and/or auxiliary lights (fog lights/driving lights).

Typically when lights are brighter than normal, the cause is related to the charging system. Specifically, the voltage regulator is allowing excessive voltage to the battery.

Intermittent problems are normally caused by loose or poor connections, although sometimes the problem can be related to internal problems. When an intermittent problem is present, visually and physically inspect all of the connections in the affected circuit.

When diagnosing the cause for dim lights, divide the affected circuit into two parts. The two parts are simply the circuit for the individual lamp and the circuit that is common to all of the lamps in that circuit. If all of the lamps in the circuit are dim, high resistance between the headlight switch and the common point to all the lights causes the problem. If only one lamp is dim, the problem is high resistance between the common point and the ground for that lamp. Suspect a bad ground or corroded connector.

Task E.1.8

Inspect, test, and repair or replace switches, relays, bulbs, sockets, connectors, wires, and controllers of parking light, taillight circuits, and auxiliary light circuits (fog lights/driving lights).

Regardless of the light circuit being inspected, there are common things that need to be checked to identify the cause of operational problems. The entire light circuit should be visually inspected for loose and/or corroded connections. Likewise the bulb terminals should also be inspected. These are all common sources of problems.

Naturally the cause of a light problem may be the lamp itself. It is safe to assume that when one bulb is not working the bulb is bad. The problem can be verified by replacing the bulb with a new one. When doing this, make sure you install the same type bulb as the vehicle was originally equipped with and make sure it is properly installed. If more than one bulb in a circuit is not working, it is very likely that the cause of the problem is not the bulbs. Check the system for an open. Lightbulbs can be checked with an ohmmeter. If the meter reading across the terminals is infinite, an open (burned-out) bulb is indicated.

Task E.1.9

Diagnose the cause of intermittent dim, no lights, or no brightness control of instrument lighting circuits.

Bulbs in the instrument cluster are in parallel so that if one bulb were to fail, the rest of the bulbs would still be able to illuminate. The rheostat in the headlight switch determines the brightness of the instrument cluster bulbs.

A rheostat is connected in series with the instrument cluster bulbs. This rheostat is operated by the headlight switch knob or by a separate control knob. When the rheostat control knob is rotated, the voltage to the instrument cluster bulbs is reduced. This action lowers the current flow and reduces the brilliance of the bulbs. The instrument cluster bulbs are connected in parallel to the battery. If one bulb burns out, the other bulbs remain illuminated.

Task E.1.10

Inspect, test, and repair or replace switches, relays, bulbs, sockets, connectors, wires, controllers, and printed circuit boards of instrument lighting circuits.

When diagnosing an instrument cluster for intermittent problems, you should look at the common ground for all the bulbs to see if it is loose. If there is no common ground, inspect the printed circuit for cracks where the power comes in from the headlight switch. If the instrument cluster is free of defects, check the circuit between the instrument cluster and the headlight switch for a pinched or frayed wire.

Task E.1.11

Diagnose the cause of intermittent, dim, continuous, or no operation of courtesy lights (dome, map, vanity, cargo, trunk, and hood light).

Intermittent problems are typically caused by loose or poor connections. All connections must be clean and strong in order for all parts of a circuit to operate normally. High resistance in the circuit causes dim or poor operation of a lamp or other component. The most common cause for high resistance is corrosion. When a controller or switch fails to turn on or turn off a component, the switch is bad or there is a short in the control circuit or an open somewhere in the circuit. A quick voltage check at the component should help determine the cause. Once the cause is identified, the type of testing needed to further define the problem will be known.

Task E.1.12

Inspect, test, and repair or replace switches, relays, bulbs, sockets, connectors, wires, and controllers of courtesy light (dome, map, vanity, cargo, trunk and hood light) circuits.

Regardless of the light circuit being inspected, there are common things that need to be checked to identify the cause of operational problems. The entire light circuit should be visually inspected for loose and/or corroded connections. Likewise the bulb terminals should also be inspected. These are all common sources of problems.

Naturally the cause of a light problem may be the lamp itself. It is safe to assume that when one bulb is not working the bulb is bad. The problem can be verified by replacing the bulb with a new one. When doing this, make sure you install the same type bulb as the vehicle was originally equipped with and make sure it is properly installed. If more than one bulb in a circuit is not working, it is very likely that the cause of the problem is not the bulbs. Check the system for an open. Lightbulbs can be checked with an ohmmeter. If the meter reading across the terminals is infinite, an open (burned-out) bulb is indicated.

Some courtesy light circuits have ground side switches. In these circuits, voltage is supplied from the positive battery terminal through a fuse to the courtesy lightbulbs. When a door is opened, one of the doorjamb switches closes. This switch provides a ground for the courtesy lightbulbs.

2. Stoplights, Turn Signals, Hazard Lights, and Backup Lights (3 Questions)

Task E.2.1

Diagnose the cause of intermittent, dim, or no operation of stoplight (brake light).

Intermittent problems are typically caused by loose or poor connections. All connections must be clean and strong in order for all parts of a circuit to operate normally. High resistance in the circuit causes dim or poor operation of a lamp or other component. The most common cause for high resistance is corrosion. When a controller or switch fails to turn on or turn off a component, the switch is bad or there is a short in the control circuit or an open somewhere in the circuit. A quick voltage check at the component should help determine the cause. Once the cause is identified, the type of testing needed to further define the problem will be known.

In many stoplight circuits, voltage is supplied to the brake light switch from the fuse box. When the brakes are applied, brake pedal movement closes the stoplight switch. This action supplies voltage to the stoplights and the collision avoidance light. In many stoplight systems, the stoplight filaments are sharing the same lightbulb encasement as the taillights.

Task E.2.2

Inspect, test, adjust, and repair or replace switch, bulbs, sockets, connectors, wires, and controllers of stoplight (brake light) circuits.

Regardless of the light circuit being inspected, there are common things that need to be checked to identify the cause of operational problems. The entire light circuit should be visually inspected for loose and/or corroded connections. Likewise the bulb terminals should also be inspected. These are all common sources of problems.

Naturally the cause of a light problem may be the lamp itself. It is safe to assume that when one bulb is not working the bulb is bad. The problem can be verified by replacing the bulb with a new one. When doing this, make sure you install the same type bulb as the vehicle was originally equipped with and make sure it is properly installed. If more than one bulb in a circuit is not working, it is very likely that the cause of the problem is not the bulbs. Check the system for an open. Lightbulbs can be checked with an ohmmeter. If the meter reading across the terminals is infinite, an open (burned-out) bulb is indicated.

Task E.2.3

Diagnose the cause of no turn signal and/or hazard lights, or lights with no flash on one or both sides.

The signal light flasher contains a bimetallic contact arm that is surrounded by a heating coil. There is one contact on the bimetallic arm and another which is stationary. When the ignition is on, voltage is supplied through the flasher contacts to the turn signal switch. This switch directs the voltage to either the left or right turn signal circuits in response to turn signal switch position selected by the driver. When current starts to flow through the flasher unit, the heating coil warms the bimetallic arm which then bends and separates the contacts. With the contact open, the heating coil and bimetallic arm cools and allows the contact to close. This opening and closing of the contact is repeated to provide the flashing action of the circuit. If resistance in the circuit is reduced, such as in the case of a burned-out bulb, current in the circuit is increased. This heats the heating element faster and therefore decreases the heat/cool cycle of the bimetallic contact arm. The result is a faster flash rate.

If the brake pedal is applied during a right turn, the left brake light is illuminated. When the hazard switch is pressed, voltage is applied to the hazard flasher through the hazard switch and signal light switch to the front and rear signal lights. The hazard flasher has the same general design as conventional flashers.

Task E.2.4

Inspect, test, and repair or replace switches, flasher units, bulbs, sockets, connectors, and wires of turn signal and hazard light circuits.

Regardless of the light circuit being inspected, there are common things that need to be checked to identify the cause of operational problems. The entire light circuit should be visually inspected for loose and/or corroded connections. Likewise the bulb terminals should also be inspected. These are all common sources of problems.

Naturally the cause of a light problem may be the lamp itself. It is safe to assume that when one bulb is not working the bulb is bad. The problem can be verified by replacing the bulb with a new one. When doing this, make sure you install the same type bulb as the vehicle was originally equipped with and make sure it is properly installed. If more than one bulb in a circuit is not working, it is very likely that the cause of the problem is not the bulbs. Check the system for an open. Lightbulbs can be checked with an ohmmeter. If the meter reading across the terminals is infinite, an open (burned-out) bulb is indicated.

Task E.2.5

Diagnose the cause of intermittent, dim, improper, continuous, or no operation of backup lights.

Intermittent problems are typically caused by loose or poor connections. All connections must be clean and strong in order for all parts of a circuit to operate normally. Dim or poor operation of a lamp or other component is caused by high resistance in the circuit. The most common cause for high resistance is corrosion. When a controller or switch fails to turn on or turn off a component, the switch is bad or there is a short in the control circuit or an open somewhere in the circuit. A quick voltage check at the component should help determine the cause. Once the cause is identified, the type of testing needed to further define the problem will be known.

When the ignition switch is on and the backup light switch is closed, voltage is supplied through these switches to the backup lights. The gear selector linkage operates the backup light switch. This switch might be mounted on the steering column or transmission.

Task E.2.6

Inspect, test, and repair or replace switch, bulbs, sockets, connectors, and wires of backup light circuits.

Many backup light switches are mounted on top of the steering column under the dash, and these switches are often combined with the neutral safety switch. The combination backup and neutral safety switch is operated by the gearshift tube in the steering column. The backup light switch might be adjusted by loosening the mounting bolts and rotating the switch.

F. Gauges, Warning Devices, and Driver Information Systems Diagnosis and Repair (6 Questions)

Task F.1

Diagnose the cause of intermittent, high, low, or no gauge readings. (Note: Diagnosing causes of abnormal charging system gauge readings is limited to dash units and their electrical connections; other causes of abnormal charging system gauge readings are covered in category D.)

Many vehicles are equipped with thermal-electric gauges. These gauges contain a bimetallic strip surrounded by a heating coil. The pivoted gauge pointer is connected to the bimetallic strip. The sending unit contains a variable resistor. In a fuel gauge, this variable resistor is connected to a float in the fuel tank. If the tank is filled with fuel, the sending unit resistance decreases, and the current flow through the bimetallic strip increases. This increased current flow heats the bimetallic strip and pushes the pointer toward the full position.

The voltage limiter supplies about 5V to the gauges regardless of the charging system voltage. If the voltage limiter is higher than specified, all the gauges have high readings. A defective voltage limiter may also cause low or erratic readings on all the gauges. The voltage limiter requires a ground connection through the instrument cluster. High resistance in the instrument cluster ground reduces heating coil current in the voltage limiter. This action allows the limiter contacts to remain closed longer. Under this condition, voltage output from the limiter increases and gauge readings are higher. Some gauges contain two coils, and the pointer is mounted on a magnet under these coils. In a temperature gauge, the sending unit is connected to the hot coil and the cold coil is grounded. If the coolant is cold, the sending unit has a high resistance. Under this condition, current flows through the lower resistance of the cold coil. Coil magnetism around the cold coil attracts the magnet and the pointer to the cold position. As the coolant temperature increases, the sending unit resistance decreases. When the engine is at normal operating temperature, the current flows through the lower resistance of the hot coil and sending unit. This action attracts the magnet and the pointer to the hot position.

Task F.2

Inspect, test, and repair or replace gauges, gauge sending units, connectors, wires, controllers, and printed circuit boards of gauge circuits.

A typical gauge circuit is no more than a simple series circuit with a variable resistor. The variable resistor or sending unit responds to the change in fluid level or operating condition of the engine. Because the gauge is part of this series circuit, a change in circuit resistance will cause a change in voltage to the gauge and in current flow through the circuit. Unwanted resistance, from corroded terminals or similar problems, will cause the gauge to read incorrectly, as will high operating voltages and defective sending units. Sending units can be tested with an ohmmeter. Specifications are normally given for the sending unit in a variety of positions or conditions. Voltage checks at the gauge may also be necessary to diagnose the gauge circuit. Sending units, gauges, controllers, and printed circuit boards are replaced, not repaired, when they are found to be defective.

Task F.3

Diagnose the cause(s) of intermittent, high, low, or no readings on electronic instrument clusters.

Many electronic instrument displays provide an initial illumination of all segments when the ignition switch is turned on. This illumination proves the operation of the display segments. During this initial display, all the segments in the electronic instrument displays should be brightly illuminated for a few seconds. If some of the segments are not illuminated, replace the electronic instrument cluster. When none of the segments are illuminated, check the fuses and voltage supply to the display. Many electronic instrument displays have self-diagnostic capabilities. In some electronic instrument displays, a specific gauge illumination or digital display will indicate defects in the display. Other electronic displays may be diagnosed with a scan tool.

Task F.4

Inspect, test, and repair or replace sensors, sending units, connectors, wires, and controllers of electronic instrument circuits.

Circuits for electronic instrumentation are very like those found in a conventional instrument circuit. When testing electronic instrument components, it is important to remember that electronic gauges can be either analog or digital. Analog gauges give the ability to show a constant change in value. Digital circuits operate in one of two states: on or off. The pulsing of the circuit (on and off) is what determines the readings on the instruments.

In order for an electronic gauge to display an accurate reading, it must receive an accurate signal from its sensor or sensors, it must receive the correct amount of voltage to operate, and it must function properly. Whenever diagnosing these systems, test the part of the circuit that is most likely to cause the observed problem.

Task F.5
Diagnose the cause of constant, intermittent, or no operation of warning light, indicator lights, and other driver information systems.

The most likely causes for constant operation of a warning or indicator light would be the existence of the situation the light was designed to warn the driver about or the controlling circuit is shorted and the switch or sender bypassed. If the warning light works intermittently, the most likely cause is a loose wire or connector. If the light does not work at all, the bulb is burned out or there is an open in the circuit.

Task F.6
Inspect, test, and repair or replace bulbs, sockets, connectors, wires, electronic components, and controllers of warning light, indicator light, and driver information system circuits.

Some warning lights are operated by the body control module (BCM). The door ajar switches and the low washer fluid switch send an input signal to the BCM if a door is ajar or the washer fluid is low. When one of these signals is received, the BCM grounds the appropriate circuit.

Some vehicles use a fiber-optic system to monitor lamp status. If a lamp is on, light will be transmitted through the fiber-optic cable to the display.

Task F.7
Diagnose the cause of constant, intermittent, or no operation of audible warning devices.

Some buzzer relays contain the seat belt and the key buzzer. If the key is left in the ignition switch or the headlights are on, and the driver door is opened, the circuit is completed from Buzzer Terminal 1 through the key warning switch, or headlight switch, and the driver door switch to the ground. Under this condition, current flows through the circuit and the buzzer is activated. When the ignition switch is turned on, current flows through the timer, seat belt buzzer, and seat belt buckle switch to the ground. Under this condition, the buzzer is activated. Current also flows from the timer through the seat belt warning light to the ground. When the driver seat belt is buckled, the buzzer circuit is open and the buzzer is deactivated. The heater opens the timer contacts after eight seconds and the light goes out.

Task F.8
Inspect, test, and repair or replace switches, relays, sensors, timers, electronic components, controllers, printed circuits, connectors, and wires of audible warning device circuits.

Various types of tone generators, including buzzers, chimes, and voice synthesizers, are used to remind drivers of a number of vehicle conditions. These tone generators should be checked for operation by running each through the prescribed self-test mode. Audible warning devices are generally activated by the closing of a switch. A tone is emitted to warn the driver that something in the system is not functioning properly or that a situation exists that must be corrected. Many of the warning systems on today's vehicles are triggered by a PCM or BCM, as are the gauges. Always refer to the testing methods recommended by the manufacturer when testing these systems

G. Horn and Wiper/Washer Diagnosis and Repair (3 Questions)

Task G.1
Diagnose the cause of constant, intermittent, or no operation of horn(s).

Many horn circuits contain a relay. The voltage is supplied from the positive battery terminal through a fuse link to the relay winding and contacts. When the horn switch is closed on top of the steering column, the relay winding is grounded through the switch. This action closes the relay contacts, and voltage is supplied through these contacts to the horns.

When the horn switch is closed in some circuits, voltage is supplied through the horn switch to the horns. A relay is not used in these circuits. Many vehicles have low and high pitch horns. Some horns have a pitch adjustment screw.

Task G.2

Inspect, test, and repair or replace horn(s), horn relay, horn button (switch), connectors, wires and controllers of horn circuits.

Like any electrical circuit, the horn circuit and its components should be inspected for corrosion, damage, and looseness. If the circuit has any defects, that part should be repaired or replaced. On some vehicles the horn has an adjustment that can be set to a desired tone. This adjustment is normally a screw. Weak operation of a horn can often be corrected through adjustment but the problem is typically not caused by a misadjusted horn. Weak horn operation is most likely caused by excessive resistance in the circuit.

Task G.3

Diagnose the cause of wiper problems including constant operation, intermittent operation, poor speed control, no parking, or no operation of wiper.

Some wiper motors contain a series field coil, a shunt field coil, and a relay. When the wiper switch is turned on, the relay winding is grounded through one set of switch contacts. This action closes the relay contacts, and current is supplied through these contacts to the series field coil and armature. Under this condition, the wiper motor starts turning. If the wiper switch is in the high-speed condition, the shunt coil is not grounded and the motor turns at high speed.

When the wiper switch is in the low-speed position, the shunt coil is grounded through the second set of wiper switch contacts. Under this condition, current flows through the shunt coil and the wiper switch to ground. Current flow through the shunt coil creates a strong magnetic field that induces more opposing voltage in the armature windings. This opposing voltage in the armature windings reduces current flow through the series coil and armature windings to slow the armature. If the wiper motor fails to park or parks in the wrong position, the parking switch or cam is probably defective.

Some wiper motors have permanent magnets in place of the field coils. These motors have a low-speed and a high-speed brush. In some of these motors, the low-speed brush is directly opposite the common brush, and the high-speed brush is positioned between these two brushes.

The most likely causes for constant operation of a wiper system would be a faulty or stuck switch or the controlling circuit is shorted and the switch is bypassed. If the wipers do not park properly, the park mechanism inside the wiper motor is undoubtedly faulty. If the wipers work intermittently, the most likely cause is a loose wire or connector. If the wipers do not work at all, the wiper motor is bad or there is an open in the circuit.

Task G.4

Inspect, test, and replace intermittent (pulsing) wiper controls.

Many vehicles are equipped with intermittent or interval wiper motor circuits. In most of these circuits, the delay is set by the driver. A variable resistor in the intermittent wiper control module provides a voltage input to the intermittent wiper module. This module operates the wiper motor to provide the proper delay. In some intermittent wiper controls, various resistors are connected in the circuit as the switch is rotated.

When the wiper switch is placed in the high-speed position, voltage is supplied through the high-speed switch contact to the high-speed brush in the wiper motor. If the wiper switch is placed in the low-speed position, a voltage signal is sent from the wiper switch to the intermittent wiper module. When the signal is received, the module grounds the low-speed relay winding. This action closes the relay contacts, and voltage is supplied through these contacts to the low-speed brush in the wiper motor.

If the wiper switch is placed in one of the intermittent positions, a unique voltage signal is sent to the intermittent wiper module. When this signal is received, the module opens and closes the ground circuit on the low-speed relay winding to provide the proper delay interval.

Some vehicles are equipped with speed-sensitive wipers. This is a system that uses a speed signal from the vehicle speed sensor (VSS), either directly or from the powertrain control module (PCM), to determine the speed of the wiper motor.

Task G.5

Inspect, test, and replace wiper motor, resistors, switches, relays, controllers, connections, and wires of wiper circuits.

The wiper circuit can be tested like any other circuit. Normally there are specifications available for available voltage to the wiper motor at various switch positions. The speed of the wiper motor is controlled by varying the voltage and current to the motor.

When checking the wiper system, never allow the wipers to run continuously across a dry windshield. The frictional drag on the glass may cause damage to the wiper motor. Wet the glass before operating the wipers.

Task G.6

Diagnose the cause of constant, intermittent, or no operation of window washer.

Many windshield washer systems have an electric pump mounted in the bottom of the washer fluid reservoir. When the washer button is pressed, voltage is supplied through the switch to the washer motor. This motor operates a pump that forces washer fluid through the hoses to the washer nozzles.

Task G.7

Inspect, test, and repair or replace washer motor, pump assembly, relays, switches, connectors, and wires of washer circuits.

When checking the windshield washer system, check for low fluid levels and disconnected wires. Then try to isolate the problem by disconnecting the hose at the pump and operating the system. If the pump ejects a stream of fluid, then the hoses are clogged. If the pump does not spray, observe the pump motor while activating the washer switch. If the motor operates, check for blockage at the pump. If there is no blockage, replace the motor. If the motor fails to operate, check for voltage and ground at the motor. This will isolate the problem to the motor or the washer switch and wires.

H. Accessories Diagnosis and Repair (8 Questions)
1. Body (4 Questions)

Task H.1.1

Diagnose the cause of slow, intermittent, or no operation of power side windows and power tailgate window.

Power window circuits usually contain a master switch or an individual window switch and a window motor in each door. Some power window circuits have a window lockout switch to prevent passenger operation of the windows. When the master switch is placed in the down position, voltage is supplied to the center contact in this switch through the movable switch contact to the brush on the lower side of the commutator. The other brush is grounded through the master switch. Under this condition, the motor moves the window to the down position. When the up position is selected in the master switch, current flow through the motor is reversed. Voltage is supplied from the ignition switch circuit breaker and lockout switch to the window switch.

Task H.1.2

Inspect, test, and repair or replace regulators (linkages), switches, controllers, relays, motors, connectors, and wires of power side window and power tailgate window circuits.

Power window circuits usually include a circuit breaker at the motor. Because the motors are subject to high current flow, the breakers are present to prevent motor damage. A motor draws high current anytime it rotates slowly. The most common causes of a slow moving window are poor window track alignment and a buildup of ice on the window.

The best way to diagnose a power window problem that is not caused by some physical interference or resistance is to refer to the wiring diagram for the circuit. Many switches are involved, and to quickly determine the problem you should identify all of the wires and connectors that are common to the system if all of the windows do not work properly. If only one window does not operate correctly, identify only those parts of the circuit that would affect that window.

Task H.1.3

Diagnose the cause of slow, intermittent, or no operation of power seat and seat memory controls.

A six-way power seat moves vertically at the front and rear and horizontally forward and rearward. This type of seat has two vertical motors and a horizontal motor. These motors are connected through gear boxes and cables to the seat track mechanisms.

The front and rear switches have upward and downward positions, and the center switch has forward and rearward positions. When any of the switches are pressed, voltage is supplied to the appropriate motor in the proper direction. The motor moves the seat in the desired direction.

Task H.1.4

Inspect, test, adjust, and repair or replace power seat gear box, cables, switches, controllers, sensors, relays, solenoids, motors, connectors, and wires of power seat circuits and seat memory controls.

Power seat circuits usually include a circuit breaker at the motors. Because the motors are subject to high current flow, the breakers are present to prevent motor damage. A motor draws high current anytime it rotates slowly. The most common causes of a slow moving seat are poor seat track alignment and a buildup of dirt on the tracks.

The best way to diagnose a power seat problem that is not caused by some physical interference or resistance is to refer to the wiring diagram for the circuit. Many switch positions and motors are involved, and to quickly determine the problem you should identify all of the wires and connectors that are common to the seat movement that is not working correctly. If none of the seat functions work, suspect an open to the control switch.

Task H.1.5

Diagnose the cause of poor, intermittent, or no operation of rear window defogger.

When the rear defogger switch is pressed, a signal is sent to a solid state timer. When this signal is received, the timer grounds the relay winding. Under this condition, the relay supplies voltage to the defogger grid. When the relay is closed, current flows through the light emitting diode (LED) indicator to the ground. After a preset time, the timer opens the relay, shutting off the grid current.

Task H.1.6

Inspect, test, and repair or replace switches, relays, timers, controllers, window grid, connectors, and wires of rear window defogger circuits.

The grid tracks might be tested with a 12V test light. As the test light is moved across a grid track from the power supply side to the ground side, the light should gradually become dimmer. If the test light goes out part way across the grid, the grid has an open circuit. A special compound is available to repair open circuits in the grid tracks.

Task H.1.7

Diagnose the cause of poor, intermittent, or no operation of electric door and hatch/trunk lock.

Most electric door lock circuits have small electric motors to operate the door locks. When either door lock switch is pushed to the lock position, voltage is supplied to all the door lock motors in the proper direction to provide lock action. If either door lock switch is pushed to the unlock position, voltage is supplied to all the door lock motors in the opposite direction to provide unlock action.

**Task
H.1.8**

Inspect, test, and repair or replace switches, relays, controllers, actuators/solenoids, connectors, and wires of electric door lock/hatch/trunk circuits.

If all the door locks are completely inoperative, check the fuse. When all the door locks are inoperative in the lock or unlock mode, test the lock and unlock relays and connecting wires. If one door lock motor is inoperative, test the individual motor and connecting wire, and check the lock mechanism for a binding condition.

**Task
H.1.9**

Diagnose the cause of poor, intermittent, or no operation of keyless and remote lock/unlock devices.

The remote keyless entry module is connected to the power door lock circuit. A small remote transmitter sends lock and unlock signals to this module when the appropriate buttons are pressed on the remote transmitter. When the handheld remote transmitter is a short distance from the vehicle, the module responds to the transmitter signals. When the unlock button is pressed on the remote transmitter, the module supplies voltage to the unlock relay winding to close these relay contacts and move the door lock motors to the unlock position.

When the unlock button is depressed on the remote transmitter, the locks will unlock and the interior lights will illuminate on most systems. Then the remote keyless entry module will turn off the interior lights after approximately one minute or when the ignition is turned on.

**Task
H.1.10**

Inspect, test, and repair or replace components, connectors, controllers, and wires of keyless and remote lock/unlock device circuits.

Power lock circuits usually control the action of a solenoid. The movement of the center core of the solenoid controls the action of the lock levers and arms. The best way to diagnose a power lock problem is to refer to the wiring diagram for the circuit. Many switches and solenoids are involved, and to quickly determine the problem you should identify all of the wires and connectors that are common to the lock that is not working properly. If none of the locks work, suspect an open to the control switch.

**Task
H.1.11**

Diagnose the cause of slow, intermittent, or no operation of electrical sunroof and convertible top.

When the open sunroof switch is pressed, the open relay winding is grounded through the switch contacts. Under this condition, the relay contacts close and supply voltage to the sunroof motor brush. The other motor brush is connected through the close relay contacts to the ground. Current now flows through the motor, and the motor opens the sunroof. If the close button is pressed, the close relay winding is grounded through the close switch contacts. Under this condition, the close relay contacts supply voltage to the sunroof motor in the opposite direction to close the sunroof.

The convertible top system contains a dual switch, pump motor, hydraulic cylinders, and linkages from these cylinders to the convertible top. When the down button is pressed, voltage is supplied through these switch contacts to a motor brush. The opposite motor brush is grounded through the up contacts. Under this condition, current flows through the motor, and the motor drives the pump. With this motor rotation, the pump supplies hydraulic pressure to the proper side of the cylinder pistons to move the top downward. If the up button is pressed, motor and pump rotation are reversed and the pump supplies hydraulic pressure to the upward side of the cylinder pistons.

Task H.1.12

Inspect, test, and repair or replace motors, switches, controllers, relays, connectors, and wires of electrically operated sunroof and convertible top circuits.

Power top and sunroof circuits are subject to high current flow. A motor draws high current anytime it rotates slowly. The most common causes of a slow moving top or sunroof motor are mechanical binding of the lift mechanisms or poor track alignments. This type of mechanical interference can cause a motor to burn up, a circuit breaker to repeatedly trip, or damage to the circuit's wiring.

The best way to diagnose a power top or sunroof problem that is not caused by some physical interference or resistance is to refer to the wiring diagram for the circuit. The control of the top or sunroof is based on the direction of current flow to the motors. Identify what parts of the circuit are involved with the function that is not working properly and diagnose those switches, wires, and connectors. If the sunroof or top does not move in any direction, suspect an open in the control circuit.

Task H.1.13

Diagnose the cause of poor, intermittent, or no operation of electrically operated/heated mirror.

Voltage is supplied through a fuse to the power mirror switch assembly. When the mirror select switch is in the left position, it supplies voltage to the left mirror motor. When the left/right switch is pressed to the left position, a ground connection is completed from the left/right motor through the switch to the ground. Under this condition, the motor moves the left side mirror to the left. Similar action happens for all other directions and the right side mirror.

Task H.1.14

Inspect, test, and repair or replace motors, heated mirror grids, switches, controllers, relays, connectors, and wires of electrically operated/heated mirror circuit.

Some vehicles have a heated driver side mirror. When the rear defogger button is pressed, the timer relay supplies voltage to the rear defogger grid and also to the heated mirror element. After 10 to 20 minutes, the timer relay shuts off the voltage supply to the defogger grid and the heated mirror element.

2. Miscellaneous (4 Questions)

Task H.2.1

Diagnose the cause of poor sound quality, noisy, erratic, intermittent, or no operation of the audio system; remove and reinstall audio system component (unit).

Audio systems typically work well, are noisy, or do not work at all. Since these units are typically replaced rather than repaired, a technician simply identifies the faulty part and replaces it. If the unit does not work at all, the problem is most likely a lack of power to the unit or a poor ground.

Sound quality depends on a number of things. Rattles and buzzes are caused more often by loose speakers, speaker mountings, speaker grilles, or trim panels than by inoperative speakers. Check the tightness of all mounting and trim pieces when this type of noise is heard.

Sound distortion can be caused by the speaker, radio chassis, or wiring. If the concern is the chassis, all speakers on the same side of the vehicle will exhibit the same poor quality. Distortion can also be caused by damaged wiring, which is normally accompanied by lower than normal sound output.

Static may be caused by the charging system or the ignition system. A poor engine ground or poor ground at the sound system components may cause static in the sound. Defective radio suppression devices, such as a suppression coil on an instrument voltage limiter or a clamping diode on an electromagnetic clutch, may cause static on the radio. A defective antenna with poor ground shielding may also result in static.

Task H.2.2

Inspect, test, and repair or replace speakers, amplifiers, remote controls, antennas, leads, grounds, connectors, and wires of sound system circuits.

An antenna may be tested with an ohmmeter. Continuity should be present between the end of the antenna mast and the center pin on the lead-in wire. Continuity also should be present between the ground shell on the lead-in wire and the antenna mounting hardware. No continuity should exist between the center pin on the lead-in wire and the ground shell.

Task H.2.3

Inspect, test, and repair or replace switches, relays, motors, connectors, and wires of power antenna circuits.

When the radio is turned on, voltage is supplied to the relay winding. This action moves the relay points to the up position, and current flows through the motor to move the antenna upward. When the antenna is fully extended, the up limit switch opens and stops the current flow through the motor.

When the radio is turned off, current flow through the relay coil stops. Under this condition, the relay contacts move to the down position. This action reverses current flow through the motor and moves the antenna downward. When the antenna is fully retracted, the down limit switch opens and stops the current flow through the motor.

An electric or electronic component with a varying magnetic field may cause radio static. A radio choke coil is connected to some components to reduce radio static. In some circuits, a radio suppression capacitor may be connected from the circuit to the ground to reduce radio static. An ohmmeter may be connected from the capacitor lead to the case to check the capacitor for insulation leakage between the capacitor plates. When the ohmmeter is placed on the X1000 scale, the meter should provide an infinite (∞) reading. A capacitor tester may be used to test the capacitor for leakage, capacity, and resistance.

Task H.2.4

Inspect, test, and repair or replace noise suppression components.

If the stator, a diode in the alternator, or a noise suppression capacitor is defective, it could be the source of engine noise. An open field winding would cause the alternator not to function. A defective alternator will usually cause a whining noise. A defective spark plug will cause a snapping type static.

Task H.2.5

Inspect, test, and repair or replace case, fuse, connectors, relays, and wires of cigar lighter power outlet circuits.

Voltage is supplied from the positive battery terminal through a fuse to one terminal on the cigar lighter. The other terminal on the cigar lighter is connected to the ground. When the cigar lighter element is pushed inward, the circuit is completed through the lighter to the ground. Current flow through the lighter heats the lighter element. When the element is hot, the lighter element moves outward and opens the circuit. On some vehicles, the lighter fuse also supplies voltage to the dome light.

Task H.2.6

Inspect, test, and repair or replace clock, connectors, and wires of clock circuits.

Voltage is supplied from the positive battery terminal through a 10A fuse to the clock. The other clock terminal is grounded. The illumination control contains a variable resistor to control illumination brightness in the clock display.

Today's digital clock has very little power consumption so there is no need to disconnect the clock for any reason.

Task H.2.7
Diagnose the cause of unregulated, intermittent, or no operation of cruise control.

Cruise control systems are often a combination of vacuum operated devices, mechanical linkages, and electrical components. Always check for mechanical binding of the linkage before testing the vacuum and electrical components. Often there is a specified adjustment for the linkage. Check and adjust the linkage before doing more diagnostics. The vacuum devices can be checked for operation and leaks with a hand-held vacuum pump. When vacuum is applied, a diaphragm should move. The unit should be able to hold any applied vacuum for quite some time. Once the vacuum is released, the diaphragm should relax and return to its off position.

In some systems, the control module and the stepper motor are combined in one unit. A cable is connected from the stepper motor to the throttle linkage. The control unit receives inputs from the cruise control switch, brake switch, and vehicle speed sensor (VSS). The control module sends output commands to the stepper motor to provide the desired throttle opening. A defective VSS might cause erratic or no cruise control operation.

Some cruise control systems have the control module mounted in the PCM. The control module is connected to an external servo. This servo contains a vacuum diaphragm that is connected by a cable to the throttle linkage. The servo also contains a vent solenoid and a vacuum solenoid. The control module receives the same inputs as described previously. In response to these inputs, the control module operates the vent and vacuum solenoids to supply the proper vacuum to the servo diaphragm. Because the servo diaphragm is connected to the throttle, the vacuum supplied to this diaphragm provides the desired throttle opening. In these systems a leak in the servo diaphragm might cause erratic cruise control operation or gradual reduction in the cruise set speed.

Task H.2.8
Inspect, test, adjust, and repair or replace speedometer cables, regulator, servo, hoses, switches, relays, electronic controller, speed sensors, connectors, and wires of cruise control circuits.

Many vehicles have an electronic cruise control. In some of these systems, the control module and the stepper motor are combined in one unit. A cable is connected from the stepper motor to the throttle linkage. The control unit receives inputs from the cruise control switch, brake switch, and vehicle speed sensor (VSS). The control module sends output commands to the stepper motor to provide the desired throttle opening. A defective VSS might cause erratic or no cruise control operation. If a cruise control cable adjustment is required on these systems, remove the cruise control cable from the throttle linkage. With the throttle closed and the cable pulled all the way outward, install the cable on the throttle linkage. Turn the adjuster screw on the cruise control cable to obtain a 0.0197 in (5 mm) lash in the cable.

Some cruise control systems have the control module mounted in the PCM. The control module is connected to an external servo. This servo contains a vacuum diaphragm that is connected by a cable to the throttle linkage. The servo also contains a vent solenoid and a vacuum solenoid. The control module receives the same inputs as described previously. In response to these inputs, the control module operates the vent and vacuum solenoids to supply the proper vacuum to the servo diaphragm. Because the servo diaphragm is connected to the throttle, the vacuum supplied to this diaphragm provides the desired throttle opening. In these systems a leak in the servo diaphragm might cause erratic cruise control operation or gradual reduction in the cruise set speed.

**Task
H.2.9**

**Diagnose the cause of false, intermittent, or no operation
of anti-theft system.**

Most common false alarms are caused by misplaced sensors or overly adjusted sensors, such as shock sensors. Most new shock and glass sensors now have two stage mechanisms where the sensor will give a warning when the first threshold is broken and will sound the alarm when the second threshold is broken. Door sensors will start to set false signals to the alarm module if they become rusted out or moving parts begin to wear out.

Many alarm systems tie into the interior dome light circuit to know when a door has been opened. Some alarm systems are tied directly into the door ajar switch or have a switch in the door for specifically detecting when the door is open. The reason for a separate switch is because some manufacturers have door handle switches, instead of door ajar switches, that tell a control module to illuminate the interior lights.

Modern-day factory installed anti-theft systems use a dedicated control module or the functions are designed into an existing module. Most factory installed systems are a passive only system, which means the system is designed only to start the car when the correct key is inserted into the ignition. The system will disable the starter system, fuel delivery system, ignition system, or any or all of these systems if the right ignition key is not used. Active anti-theft systems usually refer to a system that arms when the system is armed or when a sequence of events happens that automatically arm the system. An active system will sound the vehicle's horn(s) and disable the starter if it detects an attempt to break into one of its coverage zones. These zones can include the doors, trunk, hood, ignition, and a radio input. Some systems have active ultrasonic sound waves that set up an invisible shield to protect the interiors of convertibles.

**Task
H.2.10**

**Inspect, test, and repair or replace components, controllers, switches,
relays, connectors, sensors, and wires of anti-theft system circuits.**

An anti-theft system is normally concealed within the vehicle and therefore it is difficult to visually inspect most of the components. Two important tools will allow you to properly test the system: a wiring diagram and a parts locator guide. Make sure you treat the circuit just like any other electrical circuit and look for the type of problem before proceeding. A short will cause the fuse of the circuit breaker to blow. An open will prevent operation of the circuit. High resistance will cause the system to work improperly. All systems are unique and have a variety of sensors and controllers. Make sure you understand how the system should work before proceeding.

**Task
H.2.11**

**Diagnose the cause(s) of the supplemental restraint/air bag warning
light staying on or flashing.**

In many air bag systems, the warning light is illuminated for five to six seconds after the engine is started while the module performs system checks. The air bag warning light will then turn off if the system passes all its system tests. If the warning light stays illuminated, then there is a fault with the air bag system. When the air bag module is set to diagnostic mode, a code will be flashed through the air bag warning light. If this light should also fail, then the system may be set up to sound a warning tone through the warning chime system. You should also be able to retrieve codes for the system with a diagnostic tool.

Task H.2.12
Disarm and enable the air bag system for vehicle service following manufacturers recommended procedures.

The exact procedure for disarming an air bag system varies from vehicle to vehicle; always refer to the appropriate service manual to do this operation. Typically the procedure involves disconnecting the negative battery cable and taping the cable terminal to prevent accidental connection to the battery post. Then the SIR fuse is removed from the fuse box. After this, you need to wait at least ten minutes to allow the reserve energy to dissipate, before working on or around the air bag system.

Task H.2.13
Inspect, test, and repair or replace the air bag(s), controllers, sensors, connectors, and wires of the air bag system circuit(s).

When servicing the air bag system, always disconnect the battery negative terminal first and wait for the manufacturer's specified time period to elapse. This time period is usually one or two minutes. Never use a powered test light to diagnose an air bag system. Diagnose these systems with a voltmeter or the manufacturer's recommended diagnostic tool(s). Use of an ohmmeter should be restricted to circuits without connections to pyrotechnic devices. Since deployed air bags may contain residual chemicals, wear safety glasses and gloves when handling these components.

Sensors should always be mounted in their original orientation. Most sensors have directional arrows that must face the specified direction. Front airbag sensors are positioned toward the front of the vehicle and side air bag sensors are aimed toward the sides.

Always store inflator modules face up on the bench, and carry these components with the trim cover facing away from your body.

Task H.2.14
Diagnose the cause of improper operation of motorized seat belts.

When diagnosing that the motorized seat belt system and the seat belts are both inoperative, check the fuses, motors, and the module. If one seat belt is inoperative, check the door ajar switches, motor, module, and the front and rear limit switches for defects. Check the door tracks for binding mechanisms and/or debris that could be hindering the system. If the seat belt will not stop trying to move when it reaches the stop point on the door, check the limit switch on that door and then the module.

Task H.2.15
Inspect, test, and repair or replace motors, solenoids, switches, tracks, controllers, connectors, and wires of motorized seat belts.

Motorized seat belts operate in much the same way as power windows, except the driver and passengers have no control of the motor's action. The action is initiated by switches tied to the door and the ignition switch. To effectively diagnose these systems, check the motor's track for obstructions and damage. If there is no sign of physical problems, refer to the wiring diagram and isolate the probable causes of the problem at hand.

5 Sample Test for Practice

Sample Test

Please note the letter and number in parentheses following each question. They match the overview in section 4 that discusses the relevant subject matter. You may want to refer to the overview using this cross-referencing key to help with questions posing problems for you.

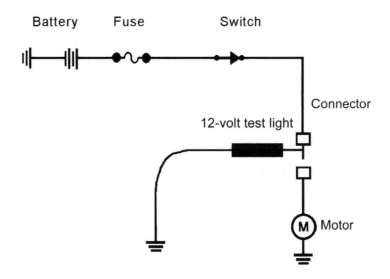

1. When an open circuit occurs at the connector in the drawing and 12V are supplied from the battery to the circuit:
    A. the test light is illuminated when connected as shown in the figure above.
    B. as connected to the circuit above, the test light will not illuminate.
    C. if the test were connected to the ground of the motor, it would illuminate.
    D. if the test light were connected to the other side of the connector, it would illuminate. (A.1)

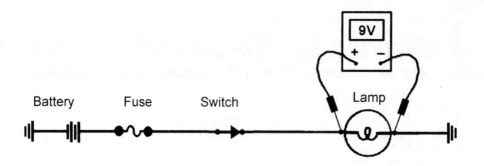

2. The battery in the drawing is fully charged and the switch is closed. The voltage drop across the light indicated on the voltmeter is 9V. Technician A says there may be a high resistance problem in the light. Technician B says the circuit may be grounded between the switch and the light. Who is right?

    A. A only

    B. B only

    C. Both A and B

    D. Neither A nor B   (A.2)

3. What type of problem is indicated by a lower than normal amperage reading when a circuit is activated?

    A   An open

    B. A short

    C. High resistance in the circuit

    D. A blown fuse   (A.3)

4. While using an ohmmeter to check the components of a motor circuit, Technician A connects the meter across the ground of the motor and motor's case to test for internal shorts in the motor. Technician B says everything in the circuit is good if there is zero resistance between the power feed or most positive point in the circuit and the motor's ground. Who is right?

    A. A only

    B. B only

    C. Both A and B

    D. Neither A nor B   (A.4)

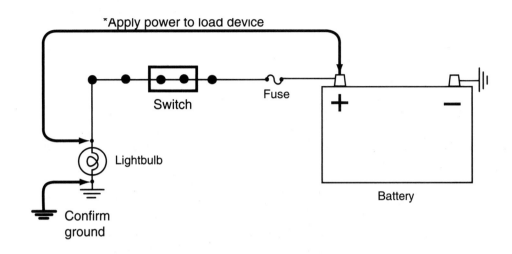

5. The lightbulb is inoperative in the accompanying figure. A jumper wire is connected from the battery positive terminal to the lightbulb with the switch on, and the bulb is not illuminated. With the switch in the on position, the bulb is illuminated when a jumper wire is connected from the ground side of the lightbulb to ground. The cause of the inoperative lightbulb could be:

A. an open circuit in the switch.

B. an open circuit in the lightbulb ground.

C. an open circuit breaker.

D. a burned-out fuse. (A.7)

6. The lightbulb in the accompanying figure is inoperative. A 12V test light is installed in place of the fuse. When the switch is turned on, the test light is on, but the lightbulb remains off. When the connector near the lightbulb is disconnected, the 12V test light remains illuminated. Technician A says the circuit may be shorted to ground between the fuse and the disconnected connector. Technician B says the circuit may be open between the disconnected connector and the lightbulb. Who is right?

A. A only

B. B only

C. Both A and B

D. Neither A nor B (A.8)

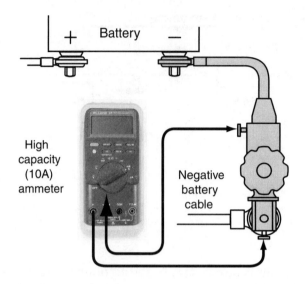

7. While performing the battery drain test in the figure:
   A. the tester switch should be closed while starting or running the engine.
   B. a battery drain of 125 milliamperes is considered normal and will not discharge the battery.
   C. the actual battery drain is recorded immediately when the switch is opened.
   D. the driver door should be open while measuring the battery drain.   (A.9)

8. A circuit breaker is removed from a functioning power seat circuit, and an ohmmeter is connected to the circuit breaker terminals. Technician A says the ohmmeter should provide an infinite reading if the circuit breaker is satisfactory. Technician B says the ohmmeter current may cause the circuit breaker to open. Who is right?
   A. A only
   B. B only
   C. Both A and B
   D. Neither A nor B   (A.10)

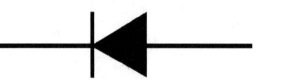

9. The symbol in the drawing is a:
   A. diode.
   B. resistor.
   C. capacitor.
   D. inductor.   (A.11)

10. When performing a battery hydrometer test:
    A. if the battery temperature is 0°F (-17.7°C), 0.050 should be subtracted from the hydrometer reading.
    B. if the battery temperature is 120°F (48.9°C), 0.020 should be subtracted from the hydrometer reading.
    C. the maximum variation in cell hydrometer readings is 0.050 specific gravity points.
    D. the battery is fully charged if all cell hydrometer readings exceed 1.225.   (B.1)

11. While discussing a battery capacity test with the battery temperature at 70°F (21.1°C), Technician A says the battery discharge rate is calculated by multiplying two times the battery reserve capacity rating. Technician B says the battery is satisfactory if the voltage remains above 9.6V. Who is right?
    A. A only
    B. B only
    C. Both A and B
    D. Neither A nor B (B.2)

12. The battery voltage is disconnected from the electrical system in a vehicle with many on-board computers. This procedure may cause:
    A. damage to all the computers.
    B. the engine to not start.
    C. erasure of the computers' adaptive memories.
    D. voltage surges in the electrical system. (B.3)

13. While testing a battery, a buildup of dirt and corrosion on the battery case, hold-downs, and terminals is quite evident. Technician A says this could cause battery drain. Technician B says the battery must be leaking and should be replaced. Who is right?
    A. A only
    B. B only
    C. Both A and B
    D. Neither A nor B (B.4)

14. While charging a battery at a high rate of current to fast charge the battery, Technician A connects a voltmeter across the battery to make sure the voltage does not exceed 15.5 volts. Technician B monitors the battery's temperature and is prepared to reduce the charging rate when the temperature approaches 125°F. Who is right?
    A. A only
    B. B only
    C. Both A and B
    D. Neither A nor B (B.5)

15. While jump-starting a vehicle with a booster vehicle, Technician A says the accessories should be "on" in the booster vehicle while starting the vehicle being boosted. Technician B says the negative booster cable should be connected to an engine ground on the vehicle being boosted. Who is right?
    A. A only
    B. B only
    C. Both A and B
    D. Neither A nor B (B.7)

16. Technician A says that a battery terminal test is performed by placing voltmeter leads between the positive battery post and the negative battery terminal. Technician B says terminal condition can be determined by measuring the voltage drop from the negative battery post to the negative battery terminal. Who is right?
    A. A only
    B. B only
    C. Both A and B
    D. Neither A nor B (B.6)

17. During a starter current draw test, the current draw is more than specified, and the cranking speed and battery voltages are less than specified. The cause of this problem may be:
  A. worn bushings in the starter motor.
  B. high resistance in the field windings.
  C. high resistance in the battery positive cable.
  D. a burned solenoid disc and terminals.   (C.1)

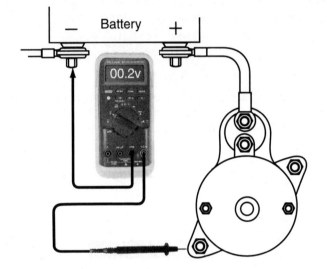

18. In the figure, the voltmeter is connected to test the voltage drop across the:
  A. positive battery cable.
  B. starter solenoid windings.
  C. starter ground circuit.
  D. starter solenoid disc and terminals.   (C.2)

19. A voltmeter connected across a starter solenoid's battery and motor terminals reads 12 volts when the ignition switch is turned to the "start" position. A distinct click is heard from the solenoid when this occurs but the starter does not rotate. Technician A says there is excessive voltage drop in the circuit between the battery and the starter solenoid. Technician B says the starter solenoid needs to be replaced. Who is right?
  A. A only
  B. B only
  C. Both A and B
  D. Neither A nor B   (C.3)

20. A car comes in the shop with a no crank and no sound from the solenoid complaint. The technician turns on the headlights and moves the ignition to the "start" position. The brightness of the headlights stays the same and the complaint is verified. All of the following could be the cause of the problem EXCEPT:

    A. an undercharged battery.

    B. a faulty clutch switch.

    C. a bad starter.

    D. an open in the starter circuit. (C.4)

21. A starter motor has been rebuilt and is ready to be installed in a vehicle. Technician A says to perform the free spin test before installing the starter in the vehicle. Technician B says to remove the terminal connector to the starter field coils before installing the starter motor to facilitate checking pinion flywheel clearance. Who is right?

    A. A only

    B. B only

    C. Both A and B

    D. Neither A nor B (C.5)

22. A customer complains that the engine will not turn over. Technician A says to first check if the engine will turn over by turning the crankshaft pulley nut. Technician B says to check the battery condition first. Who is right?

    A. A only

    B. B only

    C. Both A and B

    D. Neither A nor B (C.6)

23. When discussing an alternator with zero output, Technician A says the alternator field circuit may have an open circuit. Technician B says the fuse link may be open in the alternator to battery wire. Who is right?

    A. A only

    B. B only

    C. Both A and B

    D. Neither A nor B (D.1)

24. All of the following statements about using a lab scope for diagnosis are correct EXCEPT:

    A. An upward movement of the trace means the voltage has increased and a downward movement means the voltage has decreased.

    B. The size and clarity of the trace is dependent on the cleanness of the connection and the component or circuit being tested.

    C. A flat waveform means the voltage is staying at that level.

    D. As the trace moves across the screen of the oscilloscope, time is represented. (A.5)

25. Test results of a voltage output test are being discussed. Techncian A says if the charging system is too high, there may be a loose or glazed drive belt. Technician B says if the charging system was too low, the fault might be a grounded field wire from the regulator (full fielding the alternator). Who is right?

    A. A only
    B. B only
    C. Both A and B
    D. Neither A nor B   (D.2 and D.3)

26. During an output test using the full-field method, a 100-ampere alternator with an integral regulator produces 60 amperes. The cause of the low alternator output could be:

    A. a shorted diode in the alternator.
    B. a broken brush lead wire in the alternator.
    C. an open circuit in the voltage regulator.
    D. a defective alternator capacitor.   (D.4)

27. The charging system voltage on a vehicle is 16.2V. This condition may cause all the following problems EXCEPT:

    A. an overcharged battery.
    B. burned-out electrical components.
    C. electrolyte gassing in the battery.
    D. reduced headlight brilliance.   (D.5)

28. A vehicle's battery discharges in a very short period of time due to a shorted cell. Before replacing the battery a charging system test is performed. The engine is started and all accessories are turned off. Technician A says the charging system's amperage output will be lower than normal. Technician B says the generator's field current will be high when the engine is running. Who is correct?

    A. A only
    B. B only
    C. Both A and B
    D. Neither A nor B   (D.4 and D.8)

29. Charging system voltage is being measured at two places at the same time: connecting the voltmeter's leads across the battery results in a 12.8 volt reading while connecting the voltmeter to the generator output terminal and the case results in a 14.2 volt reading. Technician A says there may be excessive resistance on the ground side of the charging system. Technician B says there may be excessive resistance on the positive side of the charging system. Who is right?

    A. A only
    B. B only
    C. Both A and B
    D. Neither A nor B   (D.6)

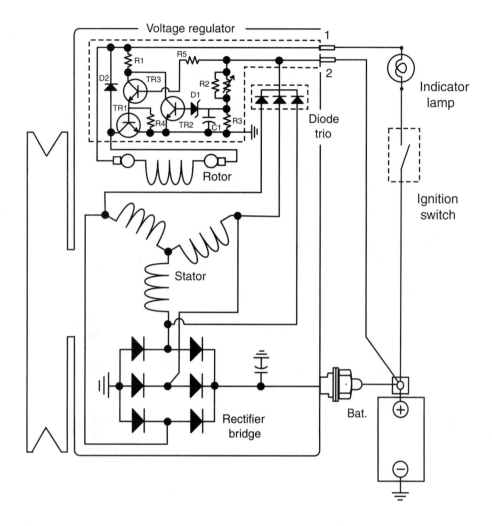

30. The charging system in the drawing has a charge indicator bulb at full brilliance with the engine running. An alternator output test indicates satisfactory output. Technician A says there may be an open in the wire from the alternator battery terminal to the battery positive terminal. Technician B says there may be an open in the wire from the regulator terminal #1 to the charge indicator bulb. Who is right?

   A. A only
   B. B only
   C. Both A and B
   D. Neither A nor B

(D.7)

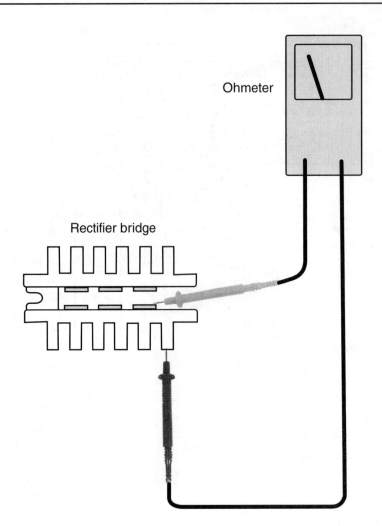

31. When testing diodes, connect the ohmmeter leads across each diode and then reverse the leads (see the drawing). A satisfactory diode provides:

    A. one high meter reading and one low meter reading.

    B. two meter readings of infinity.

    C. two low meter readings.

    D. a meter reading of 2 ohms and 40 ohms.   (A.10)

32. The headlights on a vehicle go out intermittently and come back on in a few minutes. Technician A says this problem may be caused by an intermittent short to ground. Technician B says this problem may be caused by high charging system voltage. Who is right?

    A. A only

    B. B only

    C. Both A and B

    D. Neither A nor B   (E.1.1)

33. All of these statements about halogen headlight bulb replacement are true EXCEPT:

    A. handle the halogen bulb only by the base.

    B. do not drop or scratch the bulb.

    C. change the bulb with the headlights on.

    D. keep moisture away from the bulb.   (E.1.3)

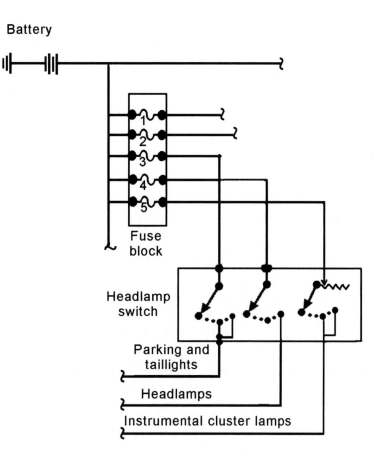

Battery

Fuse block

Headlamp switch

Parking and taillights

Headlamps

Instrumental cluster lamps

34. If fuse 5 in the circuit shown is open, what would happen?
   A. Inoperative taillights
   B. Inoperative stoplights
   C. Inoperative instrument cluster lights
   D. Inoperative low-beam headlights   (E.1.4)

35. Which of the following is the LEAST likely cause for an inoperative retractable headlight door?
   A. A defective headlight motor
   B. Loose or broken vacuum lines
   C. A poor headlamp ground
   D. A faulty limit switch   (E.1.5)

36. While diagnosing nonfunctional daytime running lights, Technician A, after some preliminary inspections, checks the circuit between the headlamp switch and the control module. Technician B begins the diagnosis with a check of the vehicle's high-beam lamps. Who is right?
   A. A only
   B. B only
   C. Both A and B
   D. Neither A nor B   (E.1.2)

37. A vehicle has one dim taillight, and the other taillights have normal brilliance. Technician A says there might be high resistance between the dim taillight and the ground. Technician B says there might be a defect in the taillight contacts in the headlight switch. Who is right?

A. A only

B. B only

C. Both A and B

D. Neither A nor B   (E.1.7)

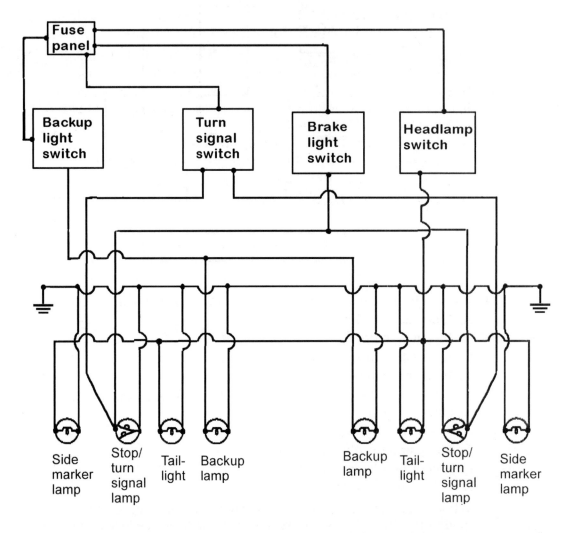

38. The rear light ground connection on the left side of the figure has an open circuit. The ground connection on the right side of the figure is satisfactory. This problem could result in:

A. inoperative LR taillight, stop light, and side marker lights.

B. no change in operation of the rear lights.

C. inoperative LR tail and stoplights only.

D. inoperative backup lights.   (E.1.8)

39. The instrument cluster bulbs are completely inoperative. Technician A says one of the instrument cluster bulbs might have an open circuit. Technician B says the rheostat in the headlight switch might have an open circuit. Who is right?

    A. A only

    B. B only

    C. Both A and B

    D. Neither A nor B   (E.1.9)

40. All the instrument cluster bulbs intermittently go on and off while driving the vehicle. The most likely cause of this problem could be:

    A. one loose instrument cluster bulb in the printed circuit board.

    B. an intermittent open in the instrument cluster ground.

    C. a grounded circuit between the rheostat and the instrument cluster bulbs.

    D. a defective circuit breaker in the instrument light circuit.   (E.1.10)

41. In a courtesy light circuit with insulated side door jamb switches, the courtesy lights are completely inoperative. The courtesy light fuse is not blown. The cause of the problem could be:

    A. an open circuit in one door jamb switch.

    B. an open circuit between the fuse and the door jamb switches.

    C. a grounded circuit in one of the door jamb switches.

    D. a grounded circuit between the door jamb switches and the bulbs.   (E.1.11)

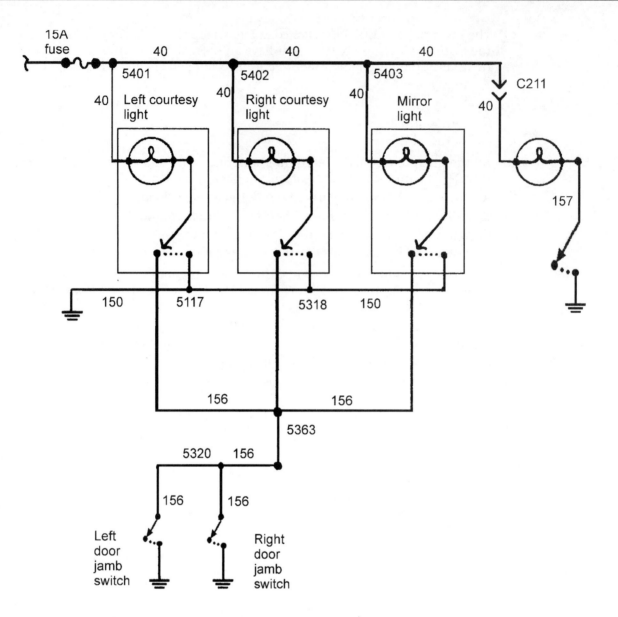

42. Circuit 156 is shorted to ground at terminal splice 5363 in the figure. This problem may cause:
    A. continual operation of the courtesy lights.
    B. no operation of the courtesy lights and lighted mirror.
    C. continual operation of the underhood light.
    D. a burned-out courtesy light fuse.   (E.1.12)

43. While diagnosing an instrument panel lighting circuit, Technician A says the power source for the lamps is provided through the headlight switch and/or a rheostat. Technician B says all printed circuit boards should be replaced if they are faulty and cannot be repaired. Who is right?
    A. A only
    B. B only
    C. Both A and B
    D. Neither A nor B   (E.1.10)

44. All of the following could cause premature failure of a composite bulb EXCEPT:

    A. high charging voltage.

    B. excessive resistance in the bulb ground circuit.

    C. improper bulb handling.

    D. cracked lamp cover or housing.   (A.3)

45. The left turn signals of a vehicle are flashing very slowly; the right turn signals are operating correctly. Technician A says excessive circuit resistance in the left turn signal circuit may cause the problem. Technician B says this problem may be occurring because someone installed a bulb with higher than normal wattage ratings on the left side of the vehicle. Who is right?

    A. A only

    B. B only

    C. Both A and B

    D. Neither A nor B   (E.2.4)

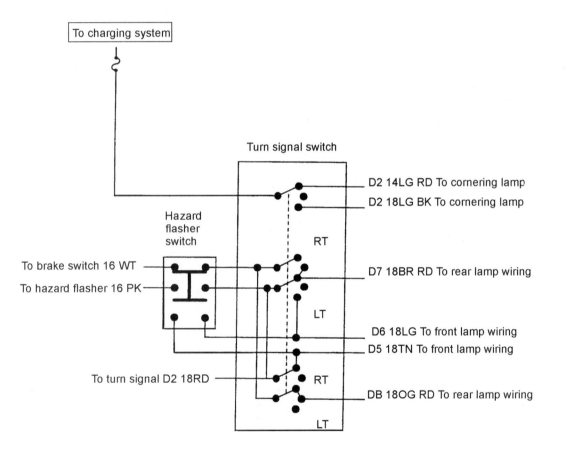

46. In the signal light circuit in the figure, the right rear signal light is dim and all the other lights work normally. The cause of this problem may be:

    A. high resistance in the DB 180G RD wire from the signal light switch to the rear lamp wiring.

    B. a short to ground in the DB 180G RD wire from the signal light switch to the rear lamp wiring.

    C. high resistance in the D7 18BR RD wire from the signal light switch to the rear lamp wiring.

    D. high resistance in the D2 18 RD wire from the signal light flasher to the switch.   (E.2.3)

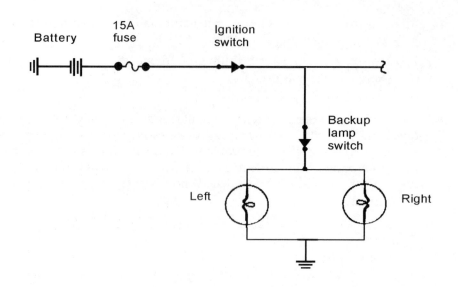

47. The backup lights shown in the figure are inoperative. With the gear selector in reverse and the ignition switch on, the voltage measured on both sides of the backup lightbulbs is 12V. The cause of this problem could be:

    A. shorted filaments in the backup lightbulbs.

    B. an open circuit between the backup lights and ground.

    C. high resistance in the backup light switch contacts.

    D. the wire from the backup switch to the bulbs is shorted to 12V.   (E.2.5)

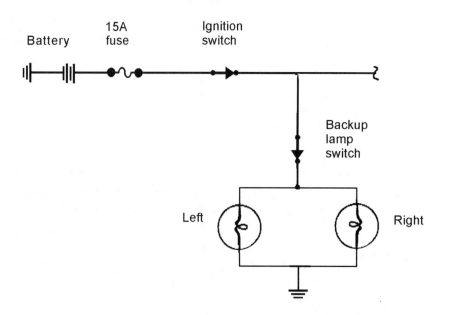

48. The right-hand backup light circuit is grounded on the switch side of the bulb in the figure shown. Technician A says this condition may cause the backup light fuse to fail. Technician B says the left-hand backup light may work normally while the right-hand backup light is inoperative. Who is right?

    A. A only

    B. B only

    C. Both A and B

    D. Neither A nor B   (E.2.6)

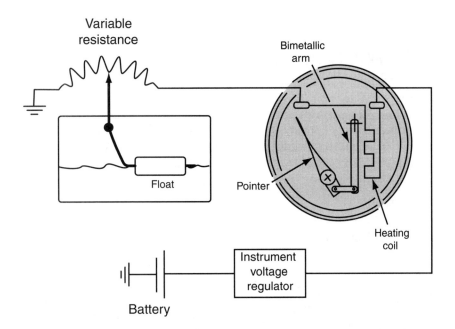

49. The fuel gauge shown in the figure reads full continuously when the ignition switch is on. All the other gauges operate normally. The cause of the problem might be:

    A. high resistance in the sending unit ground wire.
    B. high resistance between the instrument voltage regulator and the gauge.
    C. a short to ground between the gauge and the sending unit.
    D. an open circuit in the wire from the gauge to the sending unit. (F.1)

50. All the gauges are erratic in an instrument cluster with thermal-electric gauges and an instrument voltage limiter. Technician A says the alternator may be defective. Technician B says the instrument voltage limiter may be defective. Who is right?

    A. A only
    B. B only
    C. Both A and B
    D. Neither A nor B (F.2)

51. During an initial display on a digital instrument cluster, some of the segments in the fuel gauge are not illuminated. All the other segments are illuminated properly. To correct this problem:

    A. the fuel gauge segments should be replaced.
    B. test the fuel gauge circuit from the gauge to the sending unit.
    C. replace the digital instrument display.
    D. test the instrument voltage limiter. (F.3)

52. A digital speedometer constantly reads zero mph. Technician A says a faulty speed sensor may cause the problem. Technician B says the cause may be an open throttle position sensor. Who is right?

    A. A only
    B. B only
    C. Both A and B
    D. Neither A nor B (F.4)

53. All of the following can cause the vehicle's warning lights not to work EXCEPT:
    A. a burned-out bulb.
    B. a short to ground in the sending unit circuit.
    C. an open in the sending unit circuit.
    D. a defective sending unit.   (F.5)

54. While diagnosing the cause of a chime (audible warning) that intermittently and
    unpredictably sounds, Technician A says the problem could be caused by an open
    in the circuit to the warning chime. Technician B suspects that the switch circuit
    may be shorted to ground. Who is right?
    A. A only
    B. B only
    C. Both A and B
    D. Neither A nor B   (F.7)

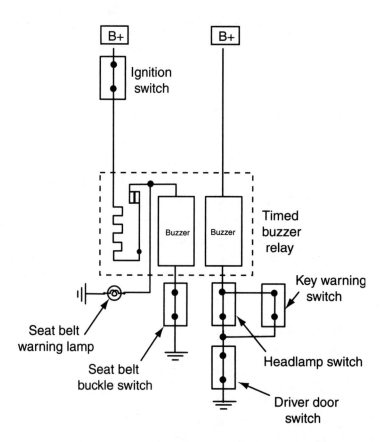

55. The seat belt buzzer and the seat belt light operate continually with the ignition
    switch on and the driver seat belt buckled in the figure. The cause of this problem
    might be:
    A. the timer contacts are stuck in the closed position.
    B. the circuit is shorted to ground at Terminal 3 on the buzzer.
    C. the timer contacts and the seat belt switch are stuck closed.
    D. the circuit is open at Terminal 2 on the buzzer relay.   (F.6)

56. While describing the typical procedures for troubleshooting a tone generator system on a late-model vehicle, Technician A says if the device does not work at all, the sounding device is bad or there is an open in the circuit. Technician B says the tone generator should be checked for operation by running it through the prescribed self-test mode. Who is right?

    A. A only

    B. B only

    C. Both A and B

    D. Neither A nor B   (F.8)

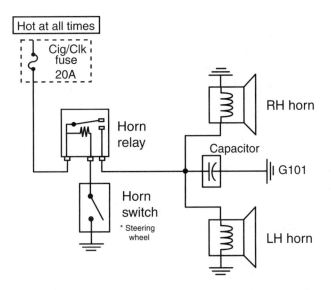

57. The horn sounds continuously as shown in the figure. Technician A says the wire from the relay winding to the horn switch might be grounded. Technician B says the relay points might be stuck in the open position. Who is right?

    A. A only

    B. B only

    C. Both A and B

    D. Neither A nor B   (G.1)

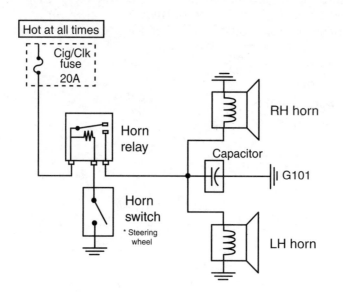

58. Neither horn will sound. The cause of the problem may be all of the following EXCEPT:
    A. an open ground circuit on the left horn.
    B. an open circuit in the horn relay winding.
    C. an open circuit at the horn brush/slip ring.
    D. an open fuse link in the relay power wire.   (G.2)

59. While discussing the possible causes for the windshield wipers operating at only low speed regardless of switch position, Technician A says the problem may be the switch. Technician B says the cause of the problem may be a worn high-speed brush. Who is right?
    A. A only
    B. B only
    C. Both A and B
    D. Neither A nor B   (G.3)

60. The intermittent wiper function is not working but the wipers move through the set speeds without a problem. Technician A says the resistance of the variable resistor in the intermittent wiper control module should be checked. Technician B says some intermittent wiper systems are incorporated into the body control module (BCM) and resistance reading should not be taken through the module. Rather, the BCM's self-diagnostic routine should be used. Who is right?
    A. A only
    B. B only
    C. Both A and B
    D. Neither A nor B   (G.4)

61. While diagnosing slower than normal wiper operation, Technician A says the wiper linkage may be binding. Technician B says there may be excessive resistance in the control circuit. Who is right?
    A. A only
    B. B only
    C. Both A and B
    D. Neither A nor B   (G.5)

62. Which of the following is the LEAST likely cause for an inoperative windshield washer system, if the windshield wipers work properly?
    A. Low fluid levels
    B. Defective switch
    C. Defective pump
    D. Blown fuse   (G.6)

63. A customer complains that sometimes her windshield washers work and other times, they don't. The fluid level has been checked and is all right. Technician A says the problem may be a loose ground at the washer pump. Technician B says the problem may be an open in the control circuit to the pump. Who is right?
    A. A only
    B. B only
    C. Both A and B
    D. Neither A nor B   (G.6)

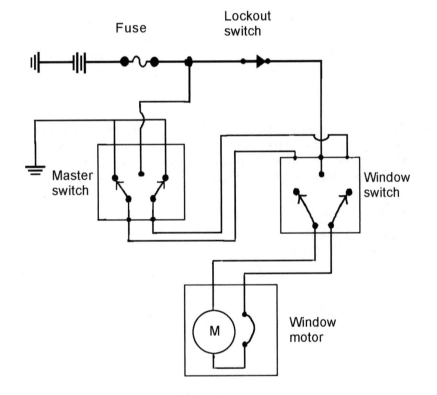

64. A power window operates normally from the master switch, but the window does not work using the window switch shown in the figure. The cause of this problem may be:
    A. an open circuit between the ignition switch and the window switch.
    B. an open circuit in the window switch movable contacts.
    C. an open circuit in the master switch ground wire.
    D. a short to ground at the circuit breaker in the motor.   (H.1.1)

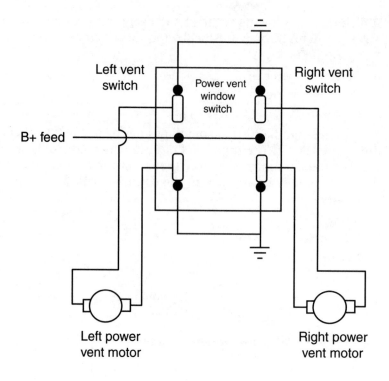

Left vent
switch

Power vent
window
switch

Right vent
switch

B+ feed

Left power
vent motor

Right power
vent motor

65. There is no operation from the RR power window in the figure. The LR power window operates normally. Technician A says there may be an open circuit between
the RR power window switch and ground. Technician B says the up/down contacts
in the RR power window switch may be open. Who is right?

A. A only
B. B only
C. Both A and B
D. Neither A nor B   (H.1.2)

66. All of the following could cause a power seat to move very slowly or not work at
all EXCEPT:

A. poor ground connections.
B. an open switch.
C. binding linkages.
D. a faulty motor.   (H.1.3)

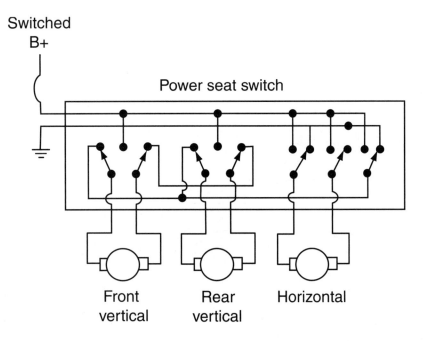

Switched B+

Power seat switch

Front vertical   Rear vertical   Horizontal

67. A six-way power seat moves vertically at the front and rear, but there is no horizontal seat movement in the figure. All of these defects may be the cause of the problem EXCEPT:
   A. a newspaper jammed in the seat track mechanism.
   B. an open circuit between the switch and the horizontal motor.
   C. an open circuit in the circuit from the switch assembly to ground.
   D. burned contacts in the horizontal seat switch.   (H.1.4)

68. All of these statements about rear defoggers are true EXCEPT:
   A. many rear defoggers are controlled by a timer.
   B. when the defogger is on, 9.5 volts are supplied to the grid.
   C. each track in the grid is parallel to the other tracks.
   D. in many defogger circuits, the timer energizes the defogger relay.   (H.1.5)

69. When diagnosing and testing a rear defogger circuit:
   A. the voltage drop from the ground side of the grid to an engine ground should not exceed one volt.
   B. a 12V test light should be illuminated at half brilliance at any place on a grid track.
   C. if a 12V test light is not illuminated on part of a grid track, the track is open.
   D. a 12V test light should become brighter as it is moved to the ground side of the track.   (H.1.6)

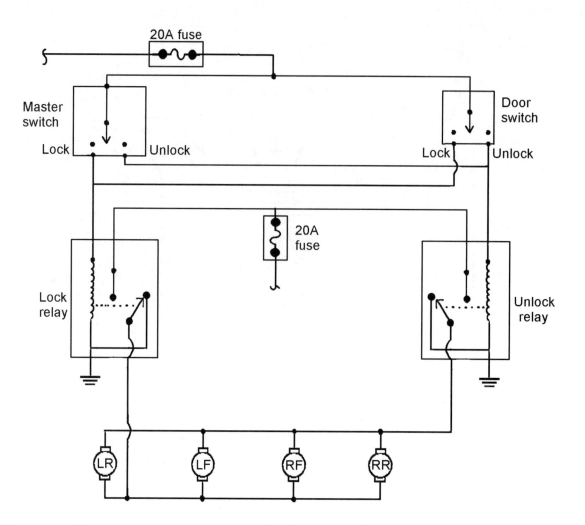

70. The RR door power lock is inoperative, but all the other power door locks operate normally as shown in the figure. Technician A says the door lock relay winding might have an open circuit. Technician B says the door unlock relay contacts might have an open circuit. Who is right?

    A. A only
    B. B only
    C. Both A and B
    D. Neither A nor B

(H.1.7)

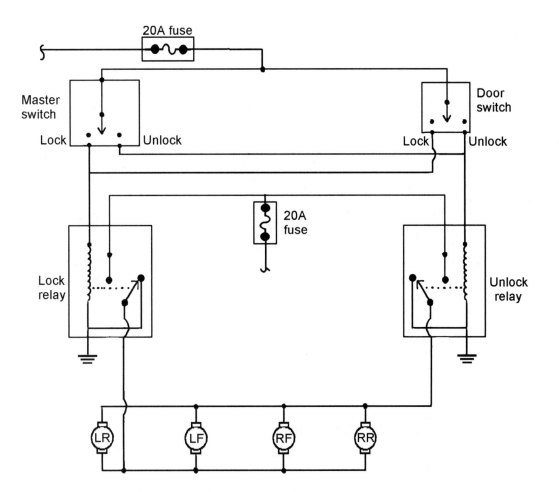

71. None of the door locks function in the lock mode. With the lock button depressed, 12V are supplied to the lock relay in the figure. The cause of this problem could be:

A. an open ground connection at the unlock relay contacts.

B. an open circuit in the LF door lock motor armature.

C. an open circuit between the master switch and the lock relay winding.

D. a failed fuse connected to the door lock switches.   (H.1.8)

72. While discussing remote keyless entry systems, Technician A says most remote controls are a remote transmitter. Technician B says most remote controls contain a replaceable battery. Who is right?

A. A only

B. B only

C. Both A and B

D. Neither A nor B   (H.1.9)

73. All of these statements about remote keyless entry systems are true EXCEPT:

A. on many systems, the interior lights are illuminated when the unlock button on the remote control is pressed.

B. when the interior lights are turned on by the remote keyless entry system, these lights go off after approximately one minute.

C. when interior lights are turned on by the remote keyless entry system, these lights go off when the ignition switch is turned on.

D. the remote control unlocks the doors when the remote transmitter is 100 yards (91 meters) from the vehicle.   (H.1.9)

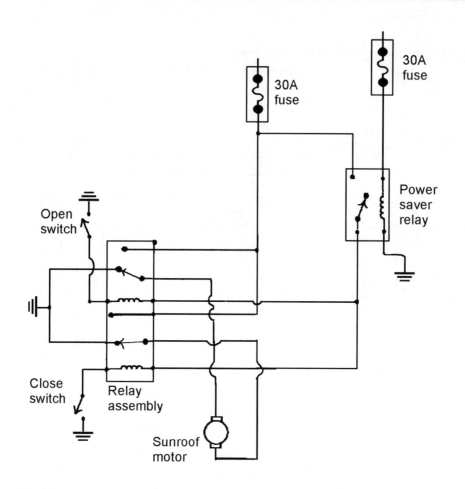

74. The power sunroof is completely inoperative as shown in the figure. The cause of this problem could be:

    A. an open circuit in the power saver relay winding.
    B. an open circuit in the close relay winding.
    C. an open circuit at the right-hand contact in the close switch.
    D. an open circuit between the close relay winding and close switch.   (H.1.10)

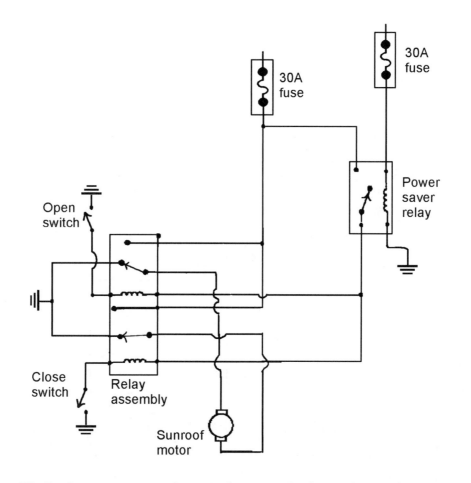

75. In the power sunroof circuit shown in the figure, fuse 17 fails repeatedly. Technician A says the wire between fuse 17 and the power saver relay winding might be shorted to the ground. Technician B says the wire might be shorted to the ground between the power saver relay winding and the ground connection. Who is right?

    A. A only
    B. B only
    C. Both A and B
    D. Neither A nor B

    (H.1.11)

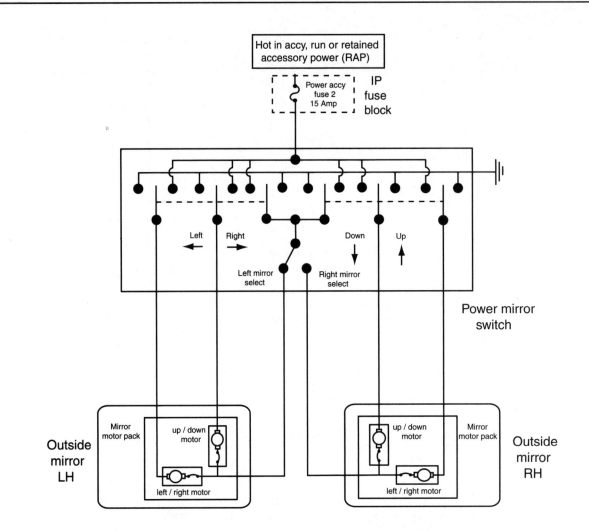

76. When diagnosing and servicing power mirrors as shown in the figure:
    A. each mirror contains a combination up/down and left/right motor.
    B. each mirror contains a separate up/down and left/right motor.
    C. the mirror motors are grounded at the mirror assemblies.
    D. when one of the switches is pressed, 9.5V are supplied to a mirror
       motor.   (H.1.13)

77. While discussing electrically heated mirror circuits, Technician A says some electri-
    cally heated mirror elements are operated by the rear defogger timer. Technician B
    says that after it is energized, the electrically heated mirror timer remains closed
    until the operator turns it off. Who is right?
    A. A only
    B. B only
    C. Both A and B
    D. Neither A nor B   (H.1.14)

78. While discussing a radio static problem, Technician A says there may be a poor
    metal-to-metal connection between the hood and other body components. Tech-
    nician B says the suppression coil may be defective on the instrument voltage lim-
    iter. Who is right?
    A. A only
    B. B only
    C. Both A and B
    D. Neither A nor B   (H.2.1)

79. All of the following statements about the radio antenna diagnosis with an ohm-meter are true EXCEPT:

    A. continuity should be present between the end of the antenna mast and the center pin on the lead-in wire.

    B. continuity should be present between the ground shell of the lead-in wire and the antenna mounting hardware.

    C. no continuity should be present between the center pin on the lead-in wire and the ground shell.

    D. continuity should be present between the end of the antenna mast and the antenna mounting hardware. (H.2.2)

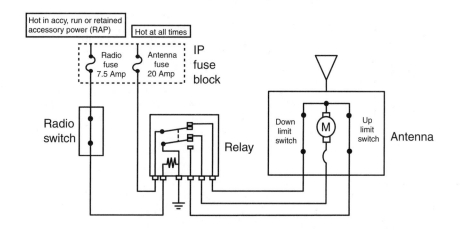

80. Refering to the figure, a customer complained the power antenna went up when the radio was turned on, but would not go back down when the car was turned off. The cause of this problem could be an open circuit in the:

    A. radio fuse.

    B. antenna fuse.

    C. down limit switch.

    D. antenna motor. (H.2.3)

81. While diagnosing a nonfunctional cruise control system, Technician A begins the diagnosis with a check of the brake light switch. Technician B checks the mechanical parts of the cruise control system before moving on to the electrical circuit. Who is right?

    A. A only

    B. B only

    C. Both A and B

    D. Neither A nor B (H.2.7)

82. A radio has a whining noise that increases with engine speed. When the alternator field wire is disconnected, the noise stops. All of these defects may be the cause of the problem EXCEPT:

    A. a defective stator.

    B. a defective diode.

    C. a defective capacitor.

    D. an open field winding. (H.2.4)

83. The cigar lighter requires repeated fuse replacements. The cause of this problem could be:
    A. high resistance in the lighter element.
    B. a high resistance connector on the cigar lighter.
    C. a shorted lighter element.
    D. a grounded wire between the lighter and the chassis.   (H.2.5)

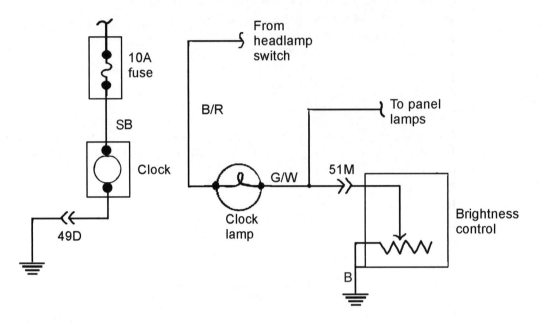

84. The clock is inoperative in the figure. All of these defects may be the cause of the problem EXCEPT:
    A. a grounded circuit on the SB wire at Connector 51M.
    B. an open circuit at body ground B.
    C. an open circuit terminal B in the clock connector.
    D. a grounded circuit on wire B/R at the clock connector.   (H.2.6)

85. When diagnosing a vehicle with an electronic cruise control and stepper motor:
    A. a defective coolant temperature sensor might cause erratic cruise control operation.
    B. an adjustment is required on the cable from the stepper motor to the throttle.
    C. the cruise control will not hold at the engaged speed; the mass airflow sensor might be defective.
    D. erratic cruise control operation might be caused by a kinked speedometer cable.   (H.2.8)

86. The anti-theft of a vehicle will not disarm when the key is inserted in the driver's door. Technician A tries the key in the passenger side to see if the system disarms. Technician B checks the wiring diagram of the system to identify the wires and connectors in the system. Who is right?
    A. A only
    B. B only
    C. Both A and B
    D. Neither A nor B   (H.2.10)

87. An alarm system will not activate when the driver door is opened. Technician A says to check the driver door ajar switch for corrosion. Technician B says to check that the interior lights are on when the driver door is open. Who is right?
    A. A only
    B. B only
    C. Both A and B
    D. Neither A nor B   (H.2.9)

88. All of these components are found on the modern-day factory installed anti-theft systems EXCEPT:
    A. control module.
    B. siren.
    C. starter interrupt relay.
    D. trunk ajar switch.   (H.2.9)

89. An air bag warning light is illuminated intermittently with the engine running. Technician A says the air bag system has an electrical defect. Technician B says this defect may cause the air bag to inflate accidentally. Who is right?
    A. A only
    B. B only
    C. Both A and B
    D. Neither A nor B   (H.2.11)

90. All of these statements about air bag system service are true EXCEPT:
    A. the negative battery cable should be disconnected and manufacturer's recommended waiting period completed.
    B. safety glasses and gloves should be worn when handling deployed air bags.
    C. a 12V powered test light may be used to test continuity between the inflator module and the sensors.
    D. sensor operation may be affected if the sensor brackets are bent or twisted.   (H.2.13)

Additional Test Questions

Please note the letter and number in parentheses following each question. They match the overview in section 4 that discusses the relevant subject matter. You may want to refer to the overview using this cross-referencing key to help with questions posing problems for you.

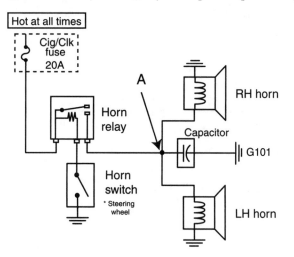

1. With the horn switch depressed, the voltage level measured at point A in the figure will be:

    A. 9V.

    B. 9.5V.

    C. 12V.

    D. 6V.   (A.2)

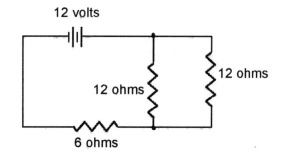

2. The total resistance in the figure is:

    A. 3 ohms.

    B. 12 ohms.

    C. 1.2 ohms.

    D. 6 ohms.   (A.3)

3. While discussing shorted, open, and grounded circuits, Technician A says a shorted winding in an electrical component causes higher than normal current flow. Technician B says high resistance in a winding causes higher voltage drop across the winding. Who is right?
   A. A only
   B. B only
   C. Both A and B
   D. Neither A nor B   (A.8)

4. An ohmmeter is used to test a fusible link. Technician A says voltage should be supplied to the fusible link during the ohmmeter test. Technician B says if the ohmmeter reading is 0 ohms, the fusible link must be replaced. Who is right?
   A. A only
   B. B only
   C. Both A and B
   D. Neither A nor B   (A.10)

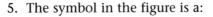

5. The symbol in the figure is a:
   A. resistor.
   B. capacitor.
   C. diode.
   D. inductor.   (A.11)

6. Which of the following are true about backup, parking, and taillight circuits?
   A. Signal and stoplights share a common bulb filament.
   B. Many backup lights have double filament bulbs.
   C. The taillight and stoplights share a common bulb filament.
   D. When the brake pedal is depressed, the stoplight switch is open.   (E.1.8)

7. Both headlights on a vehicle have normal brilliance with the engine idling. When the engine is accelerated, both headlights become considerably brighter. The cause of this problem could be:
   A. high charging system voltage.
   B. high resistance in the headlight circuit.
   C. a shorted alternator diode.
   D. high resistance in the alternator battery wire.   (E.1.1)

8. A customer complains about repeated failings of the taillight fuse. The most likely cause of this problem is:
   A. a grounded stoplight wire at the back of the vehicle.
   B. an intermittent open circuit in a taillight wire.
   C. an intermittent ground in a taillight wire.
   D. a loose taillight wiring connector.   (E.1.4)

9. The RH turn signals operate normally and the LH turn signals flash rapidly. Both LH turn signal bulbs are good. All turn signals flash normally when the hazard switch is activated. Technician A says there might be a grounded wire between the signal light switch and the RF signal light. Technician B says there might be high resistance between the LF signal light and ground. Who is right?

A. A only

B. B only

C. Both A and B

D. Neither A nor B

(E.2.3)

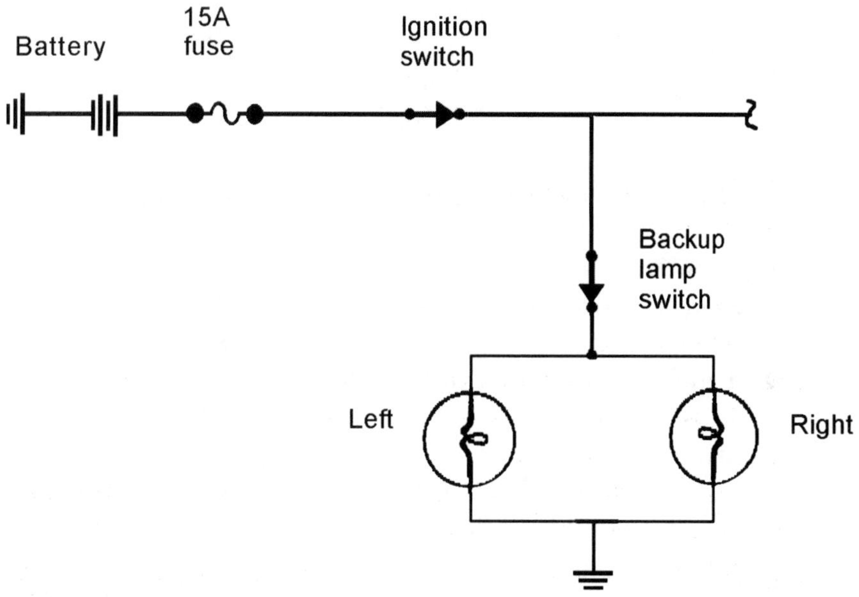

10. The backup lights shown in the figure are inoperative. With the gear selector in reverse and the ignition switch on, the voltage measured on both sides of the backup light bulbs is 0 volts. The cause of this problem could be:

A. shorted filaments in the backup lightbulbs.

B. an open circuit between one of the backup lights and ground.

C. high resistance in the backup light switch contacts.

D. the wire from the backup switch to the bulbs is open.

(E.2.5)

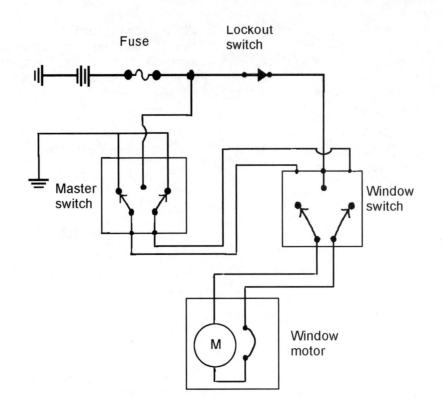

11. The power window is inoperative when turned on by the window or master switch; refer to the figure shown. The most likely cause of this problem is:

    A. an open circuit in the lockout switch.

    B. an open circuit in the master switch ground connection.

    C. an open circuit between the lockout switch and the window switch.

    D. high resistance at the window motor brushes.   (H.1.1)

12. The circuit breaker in the power seat circuit opens and closes continually without touching the seat control buttons. Technician A says something stored under the seat might be jammed in the seat tracks. Technician B says there might be a grounded wire between the circuit breaker and the seat switches. Who is right?

    A. A only

    B. B only

    C. Both A and B

    D. Neither A nor B   (H.1.3)

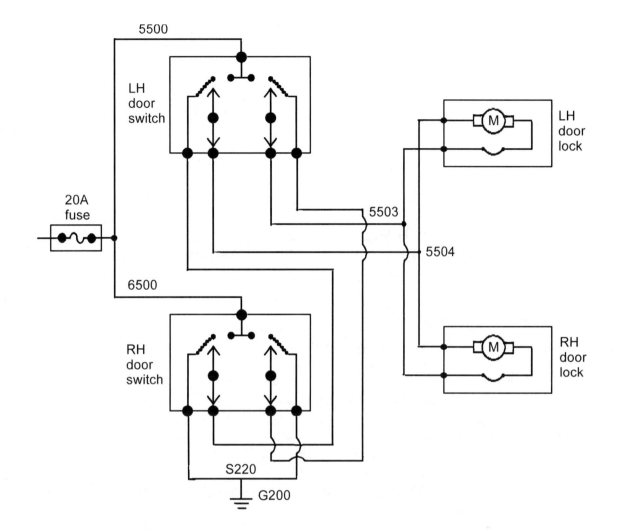

13. When the LH lock is pressed, there is no operation from the power door locks in the figure. The power door locks operate normally when the RH door lock is pressed. Technician A says there might be an open circuit between Junction 5500 and the LH door lock switch. Technician B says there might be an open circuit between Terminal C and Junction 5504 on the LH door lock. Who is right?

    A. A only

    B. B only

    C. Both A and B

    D. Neither A nor B   (H.1.7)

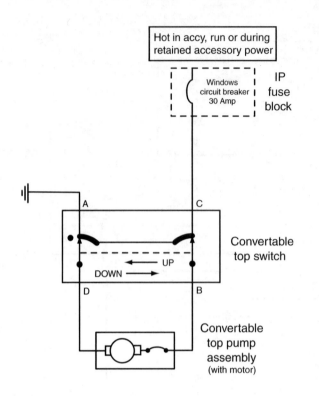

14. The convertible top operates when the down button is pressed, but the motor stalls when the up button is pressed in the figure shown. The cause of this problem might be:

    A. an open circuit breaker in the convertible top motor.

    B. an open ground wire on the convertible top switch.

    C. a jammed linkage mechanism on the convertible top.

    D. an open circuit at Terminal C on the convertible top switch.   (H.1.11)

15. The battery in a vehicle that is driven regularly becomes undercharged. The charge indicator light remains off with the engine running. The cause of this problem could be:

    A. a defective voltage regulator allowing high charging voltage.

    B. an open field circuit in the alternator rotor.

    C. a shorted diode in the alternator.

    D. worn-out alternator brushes.   (D.1)

16. In a charging system with an externally mounted electromechanical regulator, the voltage drop from the regulator ground to the alternator ground is 1.5V. Technician A says high resistance might cause an undercharged battery. Technician B says high resistance might cause damage to the voltage regulator. Who is right?

    A. A only

    B. B only

    C. Both A and B

    D. Neither A nor B   (D.6)

17. While discussing a radio static problem, Technician A says there might be a poor metal-to-metal connection between the hood and other body components. Technician B says the suppression coil might be defective on the instrument voltage limiter. Who is right?

    A. A only

    B. B only

    C. Both A and B

    D. Neither A nor B   (H.2.1)

18. A radio has a snapping type static with the engine idling. When the engine is accelerated, the snapping frequency increases. Technician A says the alternator might have an electronic defect. Technician B says the ignition system might have a defective spark plug wire. Who is right?

    A. A only

    B. B only

    C. Both A and B

    D. Neither A nor B   (H.2.4)

19. While discussing electric clocks, Technician A says that when parking a vehicle for 30 days or more, disconnect the digital electric clock. Technician B says when measuring battery drain, disconnect the digital electric clock. Who is right?

    A. A only

    B. B only

    C. Both A and B

    D. Neither A nor B   (H.2.7)

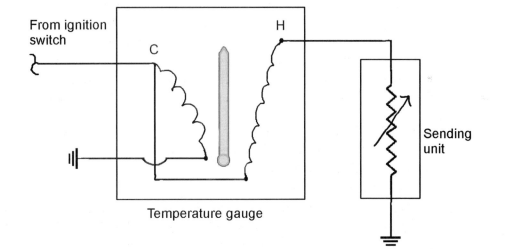

20. The temperature gauge provides a continual low reading with the engine at normal operating temperature as shown in the figure. Technician A says the wire might be grounded between the gauge and the temperature sending unit. Technician B says the wire from the temperature gauge to the ground might have an open circuit. Who is right?

    A. A only

    B. B only

    C. Both A and B

    D. Neither A nor B   (F.1)

21. During a battery hydrometer test:
    A. the hydrometer reading indicates the battery chemical state of charge.
    B. if the hydrometer readings are 1.225, the battery is completely discharged.
    C. if the variation between cell readings is 0.025 specific gravity points, replace the battery.
    D. a low specific gravity reading on one cell might indicate an open electrical cell connector.   (B.1)

22. When cleaning, servicing, and replacing batteries, Technician A says when disconnecting battery cables, disconnect the positive cable first. Technician B says if the built-in battery hydrometer indicates black, the charging system should be tested. Who is right?
    A. A only
    B. B only
    C. Both A and B
    D. Neither A nor B   (B.4)

23. When diagnosing and servicing two-speed wiper motors that contain a shunt coil:
    A. if the shunt coil is energized, the wiper motor operates at high speed.
    B. when the wiper blades park in the wrong position, the park switch might be defective.
    C. the shunt coil is energized continually in both low- and high-speed modes.
    D. the wiper switch grounds the series field coils to turn on the wipers.   (G.3)

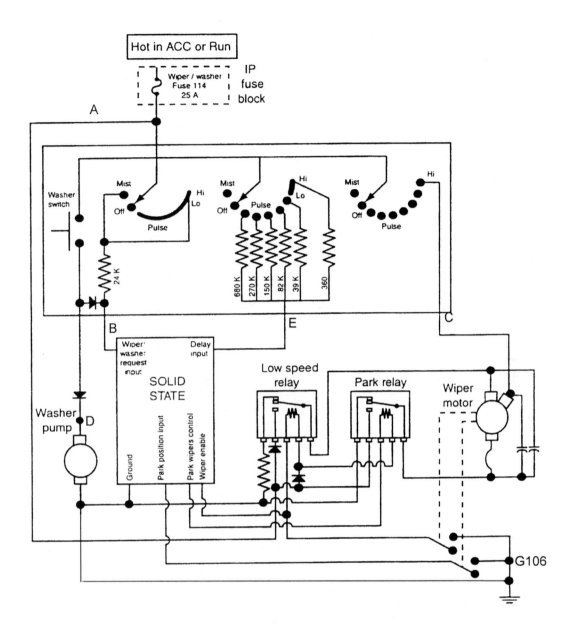

24. The windshield wipers and washers are completely inoperative in the figure shown. With the ignition switch on, 12V are supplied to the wiper switch and the module. The cause of this problem could be:

A. an open circuit in the washer switch at Terminal D.

B. an open circuit at the module Terminal E.

C. an open circuit at module Terminal C.

D. an open circuit at ground connection G106.   (G.4)

25. In the windshield wiper and washer circuit shown above question 24, the wipers operate normally but the washer motor operates very slowly. With the ignition switch on and washer switch depressed, 12V are supplied to the washer motor. Technician A says ground connection G106 might have high resistance. Technician B says the wire from terminal S113 to the washer motor might have high resistance. Who is right?
    A. A only
    B. B only
    C. Both A and B
    D. Neither A nor B   (G.7)

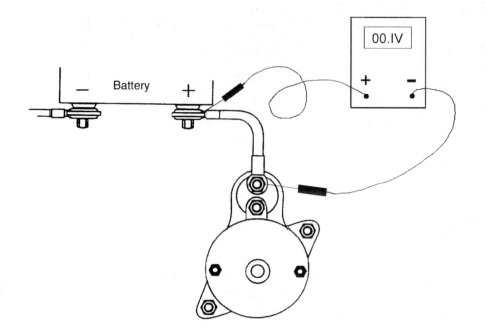

26. While cranking the engine, the voltmeter reading shown is 0.1 volt. The cause of this reading could be:
    A. excessive resistance in the starter ground circuit.
    B. normal resistance in the positive battery cable.
    C. normal resistance in the starter ground circuit.
    D. excessive resistance in the positive battery cable.   (C.2)

27. With the ignition switch off, the ohmmeter leads are connected from the starter solenoid S terminal to the solenoid case. The ohmmeter provides an infinite (∞) reading. The cause of this reading could be:
    A. the solenoid pull-in winding is grounded.
    B. the solenoid hold-in winding is open.
    C. the solenoid pull-in winding is shorted.
    D. the solenoid hold-in winding is shorted.   (C.4)

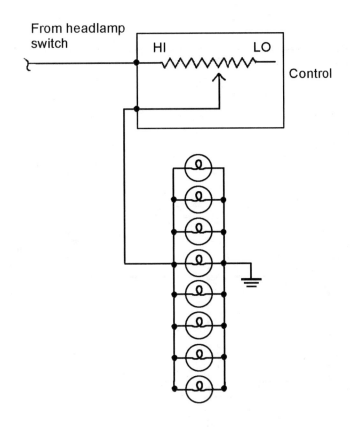

28. While discussing the instrument cluster lights shown, Technician A says an open circuit in the rheostat might cause all of the bulbs to be inoperative. Technician B says an open circuit in one of the bulbs might cause all of the bulbs to be inoperative. Who is right?

    A. A only

    B. B only

    C. Both A and B

    D. Neither A nor B   (E.1.8)

29. In a courtesy light circuit with ground-side door jamb switches, the courtesy lights are illuminated continually with the ignition switch off and the doors closed. Technician A says one of the door jamb switches might be defective. Technician B says the wire from the bulbs to a door jamb switch might be grounded. Who is right?

    A. A only

    B. B only

    C. Both A and B

    D. Neither A nor B   (E.1.12)

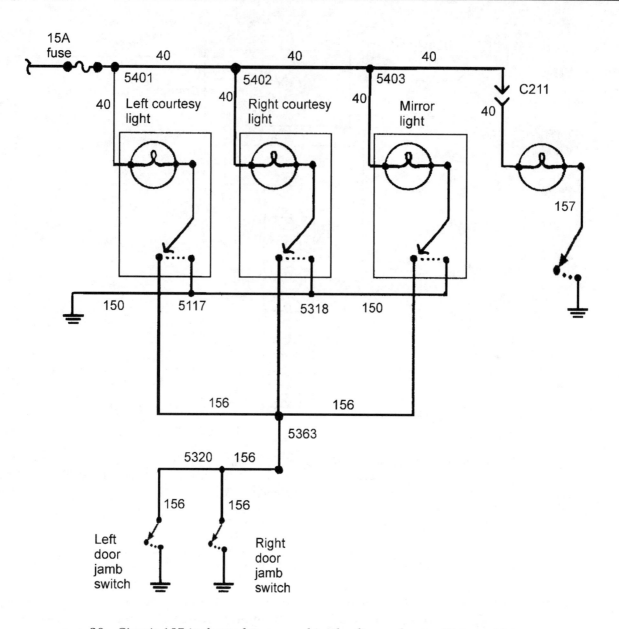

30. Circuit 157 is shorted to ground in the figure shown. This problem may cause:
    A. continual operation of the courtesy lights.
    B. no operation of the courtesy lights and lighted mirror.
    C. continual operation of the underhood light.
    D. a burned-out courtesy light fuse.   (E.1.12)

31. When discussing headlight doors with separate electric motors and a control module, Technician A says some of these systems have a manual override knob to open the doors if the system fails. Technician B says the control module reverses current through the door motor to provide door opening and closing action. Who is right?
    A. A only
    B. B only
    C. Both A and B
    D. Neither A nor B   (E.1.5)

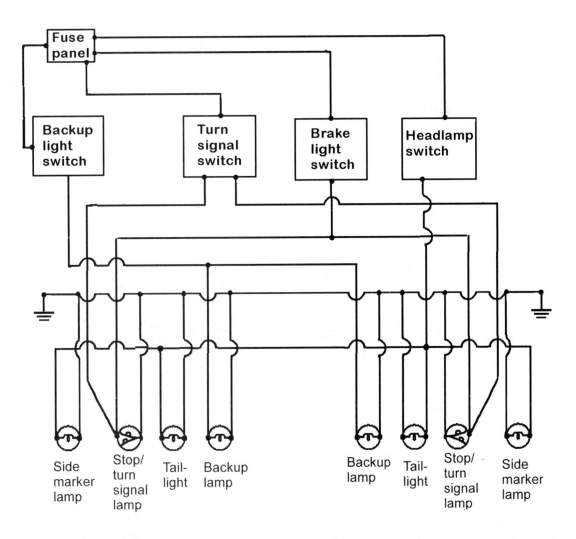

32. The rear light ground connection on the right side of the diagram shown has an open circuit. The ground connection on the left side is satisfactory. This problem could result in:

    A. inoperative LR tail and stoplights only.

    B. inoperative backup lights.

    C. inoperative LR tail, stop, and side marker lights.

    D. no change in operation of the rear lights.   (E.1.8)

33. The signal lights operate normally, but the hazard lights are inoperative. The most likely cause of this problem is:

    A. a defective signal light flasher.

    B. a defective hazard flasher.

    C. an open circuit between the fuse and the signal light flasher.

    D. a defective signal light switch.   (E.2.3)

34. While discussing the diagnosis of digital electronic instrument clusters, Technician A says some digital electronic instrument clusters might be diagnosed with a scan tester. Technician B says specific gauge displays indicate certain defects in some digital electronic clusters. Who is right?

    A. A only

    B. B only

    C. Both A and B

    D. Neither A nor B   (F.3)

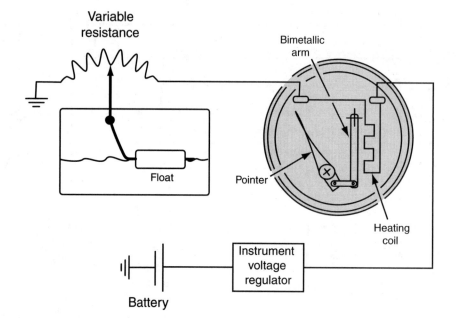

35. A thermal-electric type fuel gauge reads three-fourths full when the fuel tank is full of gasoline as shown in the figure. The cause of this problem could be:

    A. high resistance in the fuel tank sending unit ground circuit.

    B. low resistance in the fuel tank sending unit.

    C. a grounded wire between the gauge and the tank.

    D. an open wire between the gauge and the tank.   (F.1)

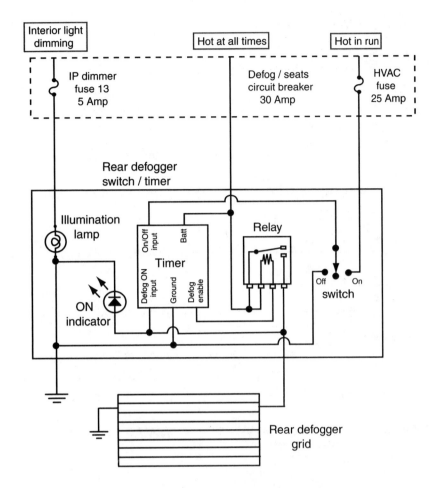

36. When the rear defogger switch is turned on, the rear defogger light is illuminated, but there is no defogger grid operation as shown in the figure. The cause of this problem could be:

    A. an open defogger relay winding.

    B. an open circuit at the defogger relay contacts.

    C. an open circuit between the switch/timer and the grid.

    D. a defective defogger on/off switch. (H.1.5)

37. When testing a radio antenna with an ohmmeter, Technician A says there should be no continuity between the antenna mast and the center pin on the lead-in wire. Technician B says there should be no continuity between the ground shell on the lead-in wire and the antenna mounting hardware. Who is right?

    A. A only

    B. B only

    C. Both A and B

    D. Neither A nor B (H.2.2)

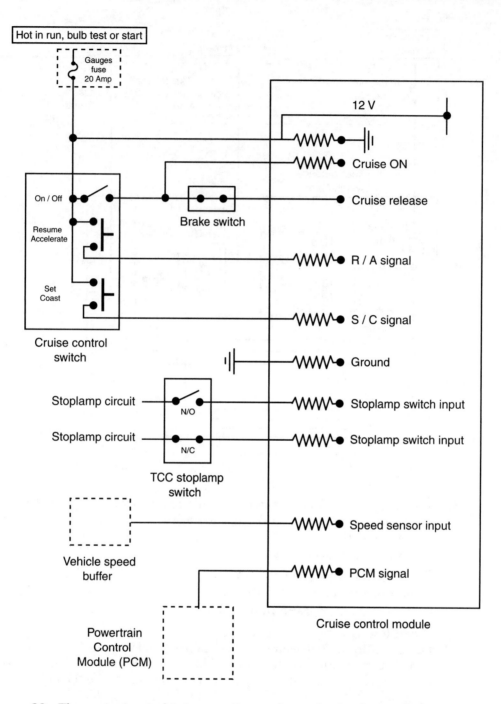

38. The cruise control is inoperative as shown in the figure. Technician A says the vehicle speed sensor might be defective. Technician B says the 20 ampere gauge fuse might be defective. Who is right?

    A. A only

    B. B only

    C. Both A and B

    D. Neither A nor B

                                                                                (H.2.8)

39. An anti-theft system has common false alarms. Which of these should the technician check first?
    A. Shock sensor
    B. Door ajar sensor
    C. Trunk ajar switch
    D. Hood ajar switch   (H.2.9)

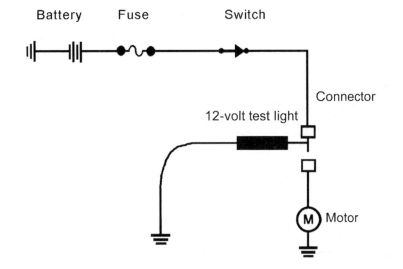

40. When the open circuit at the connector shown is repaired and the switch is closed, Technician A says the 12V test light should be illuminated when it is connected from the motor ground brush to ground. Technician B says the 12V test light should be illuminated at partial brilliance when it is connected from the input motor brush to ground. Who is right?
    A. A only
    B. B only
    C. Both A and B
    D. Neither A nor B   (A.1)

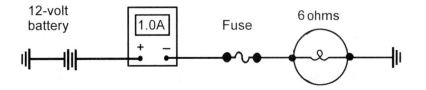

41. The current flow indicated on the ammeter shown is 1 ampere and the specified current flow is 2 amperes. The cause of this problem could be:
    A. low resistance in the light filament.
    B. high resistance at one of the light terminals.
    C. the circuit is grounded between the fuse and the light.
    D. the circuit is open between the light and ground.   (A.3)

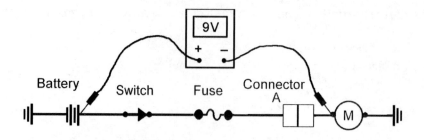

42. The voltmeter in the circuit shown reads 9 volts. Technician A says that there could be high resistance in connector A. Technician B says that there could be high resistance in the switch. Who is right?
    A. A only
    B. B only
    C. Both A and B
    D. Neither A nor B   (A.2)

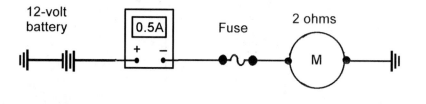

43. The current reading in the circuit shown equals 0.5 amps. Technician A says that this indicates high circuit resistance. Technician B says that there may be corrosion in one of the circuit connections. Who is right?
    A. A only
    B. B only
    C. Both A and B
    D. Neither A nor B   (A.3)

44. Technician A says that a jumper wire can be used to test power circuits for shorts to ground. Technician B says that a jumper wire can be used to test a circuit for an open. Who is right?
    A. A only
    B. B only
    C. Both A and B
    D. Neither A nor B   (A.7)

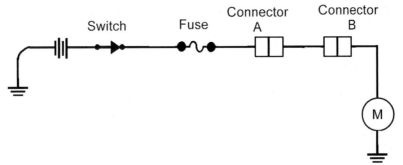

45. The needle on the device shown moves back and forth as it passes over Connector A and stops moving as it passes over Connector B. Technician A says that there is a short to ground at Connector B. Technician B says that there is an open at Connector B. Who is right?

    A. A only
    B. B only
    C. Both A and B
    D. Neither A nor B   (A.8)

46. While performing a parasitic drain test, a technician finds a draw of 500mA. After removing the connector to the trunk lamp, the technician finds a draw of 300mA. Technician A says that the trunk lamp is staying on after it is closed. Technician B says that there is another parasitic draw. Who is right?

    A. A only
    B. B only
    C. Both A and B
    D. Neither A nor B   (A.9)

47. A test light connected to ground does not illuminate when touched to either side of a fuse in the fuse box. Technician A says that the fuse is open. Technician B says that there is no power to the fuse. Who is right?

    A. A only
    B. B only
    C. Both A and B
    D. Neither A nor B   (A.10)

48. Technician A says that battery state of charge can be tested using a voltmeter. Technician B says that a hydrometer reading must be corrected based upon temperature. Who is right?

    A. A only
    B. B only
    C. Both A and B
    D. Neither A nor B   (B.1)

49. The rate at which a technician should charge a battery depends upon all of the following EXCEPT:
    A. battery state of charge.
    B. battery temperature.
    C. results of the battery leakage test.
    D. battery capacity.   (B.5)

50. When jump-starting a battery:
    A. when connecting the cables, the negative terminals of the jumper cables should be connected first.
    B. when removing the cables, the negative terminals should be removed last.
    C. never remove the cables until after the engines on both vehicles have been turned off.
    D. never allow the two vehicles to be in physical contact with each other.   (B.7)

51. A vehicle cranks slowly during starting, and current draw is high. Technician A says that this could be caused by worn starter brushes. Technician B says that this could be caused by high resistance in the battery ground cable. Who is right?
    A. A only
    B. B only
    C. Both A and B
    D. Neither A nor B   (C.1)

52. When performing a voltage drop test on the negative (ground) side of the starter circuit, a reading of 1.5 volts is obtained. All of the following could cause this result except:
    A. a corroded negative battery terminal.
    B. a loose ground connection at the motor.
    C. high resistance in the starter field windings.
    D. an improperly mounted starter.   (C.2)

53. A starter motor fails to run when the key is turned to the start position. Technician A says that an open in the starter solenoid control circuit could be the cause. Technician B says that a poor connection at the battery positive terminal could be the cause. Who is right?
    A. A only
    B. B only
    C. Both A and B
    D. Neither A nor B   (C.3)

54. A starter motor makes a high-pitched whine after the engine is started and the ignition key is released to the run position. Technician A says that the starter motor could be improperly shimmed. Technician B says that the clearance between the pinion gear and ring gear is excessive. Who is right?
    A. A only
    B. B only
    C. Both A and B
    D. Neither A nor B   (C.5)

55. A vehicle cranks slowly during starting, and current draw is low. Technician A says that low engine compression could be the cause. Technician B says that corroded battery terminals could be the cause. Who is right?
    A. A only
    B. B only
    C. Both A and B
    D. Neither A nor B   (C.1)

56. Technician A says that when installing an alternator, the belt should be able to be distorted approximately 2 inches when it is properly tightened. Technician B says that the only way to insure that a belt is properly tightened is to use a belt tension gauge. Who is right?
    A. A only
    B. B only
    C. Both A and B
    D. Neither A nor B   (D.2)

57. During an alternator output test, the technician should do all of the following EXCEPT:
    A. run the engine at between 1,500 and 2,000 rpm.
    B. turn on all vehicle accessories.
    C. adjust the carbon pile until the highest amperage output reading is obtained.
    D. clamp the inductive pickup lead around all negative battery leads.   (D.3)

58. A full field test is performed on a vehicle with an internal regulator. Technician A says that if the output is within specifications, a faulty regulator may be the cause. Technician B says that an alternator should never be full-fielded for more than 30 seconds. Who is right?
    A. A only
    B. B only
    C. Both A and B
    D. Neither A nor B   (D.4)

59. A fusible link at the alternator is suspected to be open. Technician A says that battery voltage should be present at both sides of the fusible link. Technician B says that a replacement fusible link should never be longer than 9 inches. Who is right?
    A. A only
    B. B only
    C. Both A and B
    D. Neither A nor B   (D.7)

60. A composite headlight bulb is being replaced. Technician A says that touching the bulb with your finger may shorten its life. Technician B says that dielectric grease should be used to coat the connector terminals Who is right?
    A. A only
    B. B only
    C. Both A and B
    D. Neither A nor B   (E.1.3)

61. A vacuum controlled retractable headlight system is being discussed. Technician A says that a jumped timing belt may cause poor operation of the system. Technician B says that most systems use vacuum to hold the door open. Who is right?
    A. A only
    B. B only
    C. Both A and B
    D. Neither A nor B   (E.1.5)

62. An instrument panel lightbulb does not illuminate. Technician A says that an open in the headlight switch could be the cause. Technician B says that an open in the printed circuit ground connection could be the cause. Who is right?

A. A only

B. B only

C. Both A and B

D. Neither A nor B   (E.1.8)

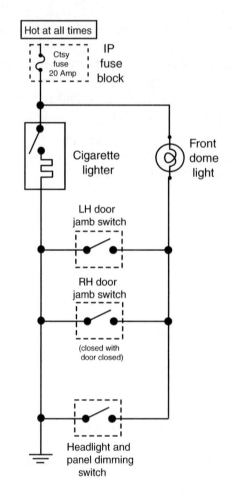

63. Diagnose the following problem using the diagram shown. The dome and courtesy lamp dimly illuminate when the cigar lighter is pushed in. The cigar lighter never gets hot enough to pop out. What is the most likely cause?

A. A door open switch shorted to ground

B. An open cigar lighter fuse

C. A stoplight switch shorted to ground

D. An open in the cigar lighter resistor   (E.1.11)

64. Technician A says that some brake light switches use brake fluid pressure to turn on the stop lamps. Technician B says that if the brake lights are inoperative, the brake light switch may be the cause. Who is right?

A. A only

B. B only

C. Both A and B

D. Neither A nor B   (E.2.1)

65. A technician adds side turn signal lamps to a vehicle and wires them in parallel to the existing rear indicator lights. Technician A says that this could cause the signal light fuse to blow. Technician B says that this could cause the indicator lights to flash more slowly. Who is right?

A. A only

B. B only

C. Both A and B

D. Neither A nor B   (E.2.3)

66. The backup lights on a vehicle do not illuminate. Technician A says that if the backup lights are wired in parallel, a burned-out bulb could be the cause. Technician B says that an open in the ignition switched power circuit could be the cause. Who is right?

A. A only

B. B only

C. Both A and B

D. Neither A nor B   (E.2.5)

67. A thermal-electric fuel gauge always reads empty. Which of the following is the LEAST likely cause?

A. An open in the gauge power supply circuit

B. An open in the gauge heating circuit

C. A heavily corroded connection to the fuel level sending unit

D. A short to ground between the gauge and the sending unit   (F.1)

68. Analog gauges are being discussed. Technician A says that gauge circuits that use an IVR will produce inaccurate readings if the alternator is overcharging. Technician B says that a sending unit on a vehicle without an IVR can be tested by grounding the sending unit wire. Who is right?

A. A only

B. B only

C. Both A and B

D. Neither A nor B   (F.1)

69. The fiber-optic left turn signal indicator does not illuminate even though the exterior lamps are functional. What is the most likely cause?

A. The instrument panel printed circuit board is open.

B. The fiber-optic cable is broken.

C. A faulty flasher unit

D. An open (blown) turn signal indicator bulb   (F.6)

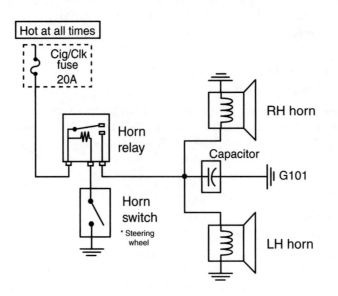

70. The horn shown in the diagram does not operate. Technician A says that an open winding in the horn relay may be the cause. Technician B says that a shorted horn switch may be the cause. Who is right?

    A. A only
    B. B only
    C. Both A and B
    D. Neither A nor B   (G.1)

71. A vehicle with speed sensitive wipers is being discussed. The wipers do not change speed as vehicle speed increases, but otherwise operate normally. Technician A says that the wiper motor may be defective. Technician B says that the vehicle speed sensor (VSS) may be defective. Who is right?

    A. A only
    B. B only
    C. Both A and B
    D. Neither A nor B   (G.4)

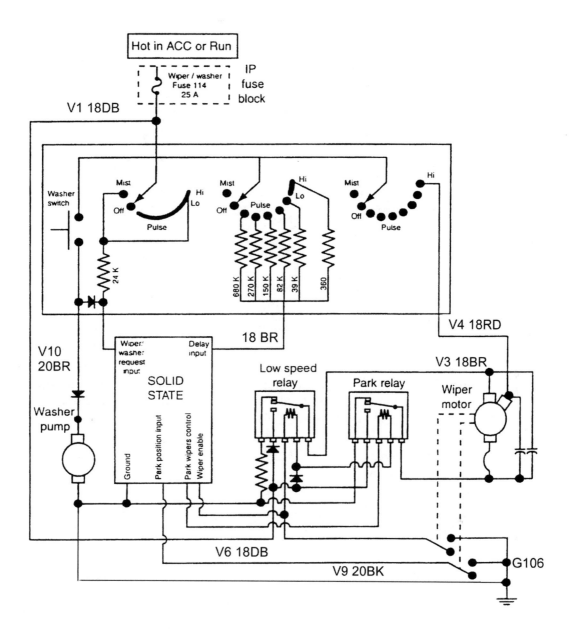

72. The windshield washer pump in the diagram does not operate. What is the LEAST likely cause?

    A. An open in circuit V10 (20 BR)

    B. An open in circuit V1 (18 DB)

    C. An open in circuit V6 (18 DB)

    D. A short to ground in circuit V9 (20 BK)

    (G.7)

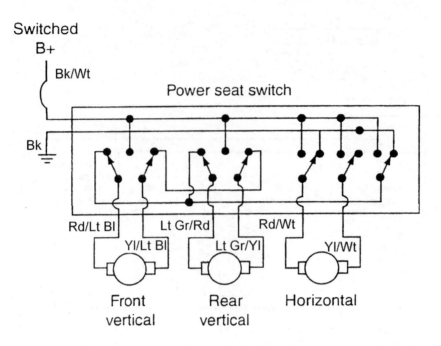

Switched
B+

Bk/Wt

Power seat switch

Bk

Rd/Lt Bl   Lt Gr/Rd   Rd/Wt

YI/Lt Bl   Lt Gr/YI   YI/Wt

Front   Rear   Horizontal
vertical   vertical

73. The rear height motor in the power seat shown does not operate. Technician A
    says that, during normal operation, there should be twelve volts at the Rd/Lt Gn
    wire near the motor when the motor is moving up. Technician B says that an
    open in the Yl/Lt Gn wire could be the cause. Who is right?

    A. A only

    B. B only

    C. Both A and B

    D. Neither A nor B   (H.1.3)

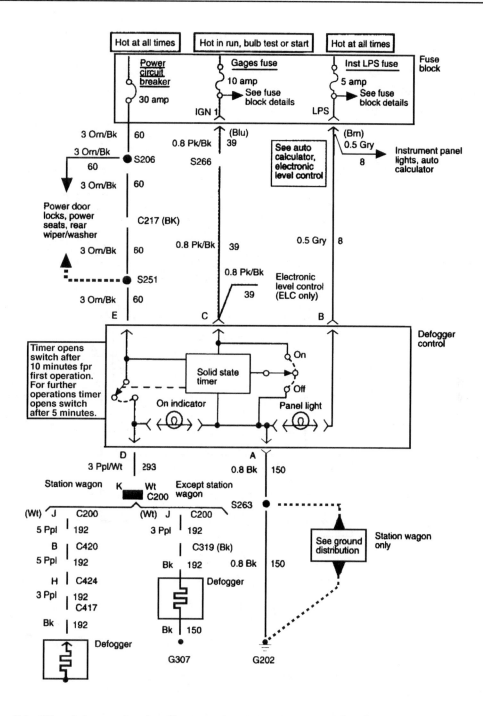

74. The defogger in the diagram does not operate and is being tested. Seven volts are found at pin A of the defogger control. Technician A says that there should be seven volts at pin D of the defogger control. Technician B says that there is high resistance in circuit 150 (Bk). Who is right?

    A. A only
    B. B only
    C. Both A and B
    D. Neither A nor B

    (H.1.5)

75. Power door locks are being discussed. Technician A says that some power door locks are operated by electric solenoids. Technician B says that some power door locks are operated by permanent magnet motors. Who is right?

    A. A only
    B. B only
    C. Both A and B
    D. Neither A nor B   (H.1.7)

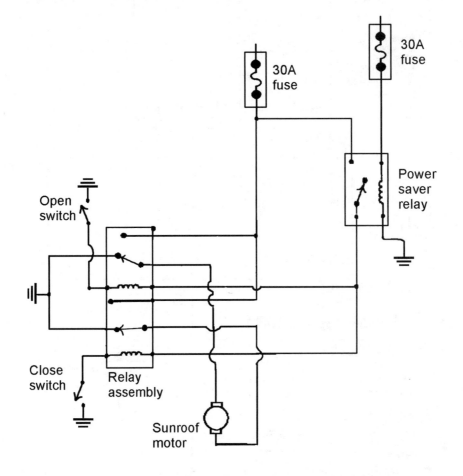

76. The sunroof in the diagram opened but failed to close. Which of the following is the most likely cause?

    A. A shorted close switch
    B. An open in the close relay control circuit
    C. An open in the power saver relay control circuit
    D. Fuse 7 is open (blown).   (H.1.11)

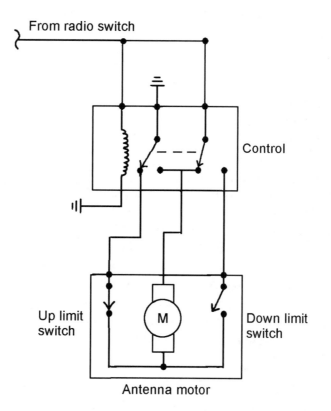

From radio switch

Control

Up limit
switch

M

Down limit
switch

Antenna motor

77. The power antenna in the diagram is being discussed. Technician A says that the antenna uses a dual-throw relay. Technician B says that an open in the down limit switch would prevent the antenna from moving up. Who is right?

A. A only

B. B only

C. Both A and B

D. Neither A nor B   (H.2.3)

78. The starter motor has been rebuilt and is ready to install in the vehicle. Technician A performs a free spin test before installing the starter into the vehicle. Technician B says to check the pinion to flywheel clearance before installing the starter. Who is right?

A. A only

B. B only

C. Both A and B

D. Neither A nor B   (C.5)

79. Technician A says full fielding means the field windings are constantly energized with full battery voltage. Technician B says full fielding should only be done if the charging system passes the output test. Who is right?

A. A only

B. B only

C. Both A and B

D. Neither A nor B   (D.4)

80. The left rear and right rear taillights and the left rear brake light of a vehicle are dim whenever the brake pedal is depressed; however, the right rear brake light operates at the correct brightness. Technician A says the left rear taillight and brake light may have a poor ground connection. Technician B says the brake light switch may have excessive resistance. Who is right?
    A. Technician A
    B. Technician B
    C. Both A and B
    D. Neither A nor B   (E.2.1)

81. The horn of a vehicle equipped with a horn relay sounds weak and distorted whenever it is activated. Which of the following is the LEAST likely cause of this problem?
    A. High resistance in the relay load circuit
    B. High resistance in the horn ground circuit
    C. Excessive voltage drop between the relay load contact and the horn
    D. Excessive voltage drop across the relay coil winding   (G.2)

82. The circuit breaker that protects an electric window circuit blows whenever an attempt is made to lower the window. Technician A says the internal resistance of the motor is too high. Technician B says the window regulator may be sticking. Who is right?
    A. Technician A
    B. Technician B
    C. Both A and B
    D. Neither A nor B   (H.1.1)

83. All of the following could cause a slow cranking condition EXCEPT:
    A. overadvanced ignition timing.
    B. shorted neutral safety switch.
    C. misaligned starter mounting.
    D. low battery state of charge.   (C.6)

84. A customer complains that occasionally he is unable to start his engine. The engine begins to crank at normal speed and then suddenly a "whee" noise is heard and the engine stops cranking. Technician A says the starter drive may be slipping. Technician B says there may be excessive voltage drop across the starter solenoid contacts. Who is right?
    A. Technician A
    B. Technician B
    C. Both A and B
    D. Neither A nor B   (C.3)

85. A vehicle with a no crank condition is being tested. When the battery and start terminals on the starter's solenoid are connected with a jumper wire, the starter begins to crank the engine. Technician A says the starter solenoid may be bad. Technician B says the ignition switch may be bad. Who is right?
    A. Technician A
    B. Technician B
    C. Both A and B
    D. Neither A nor B   (C.4)

86. The turn signals of a vehicle are inoperative. The green indicator bulbs in the dash do not turn on when the turn signal switch is placed in either the right or left turn position. Technician A says the turn signal flasher contacts may have fused together. Technician B says the circuit from the turn signal flasher to the turn signal switch may be open. Who is right?
    A. Technician A
    B. Technician B
    C. Both A and B
    D. Neither A nor B

    (E.2.3)

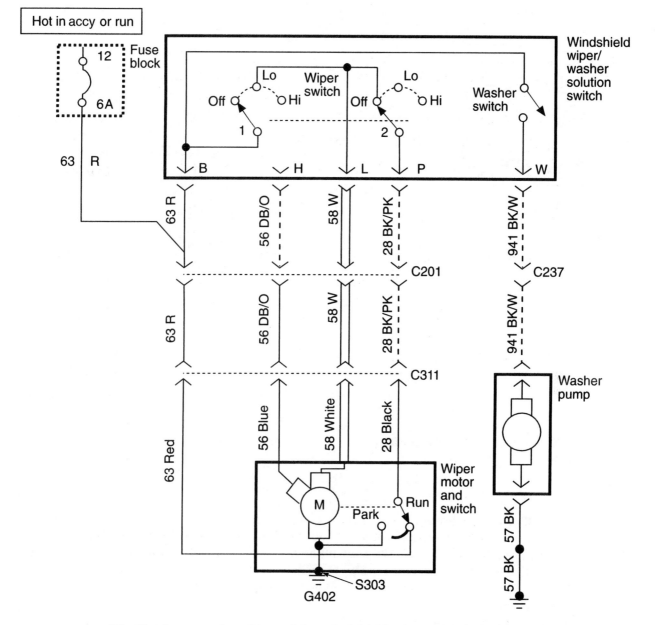

87. The low-speed position of the windshield wiper system shown in the figure does not work; the high speed position works normally. Technician A says circuit 58 may be open. Technician B says circuit 63 may be open. Who is right?
    A. Technician A
    B. Technician B
    C. Both A and B
    D. Neither A nor B

    (G.3)

88. A voltmeter that is connected across the input and output terminals of an instrument cluster illumination lamp rheostat (dimmer control) indicates 12.6 volts with the switch in the maximum brightness position and the engine off. Which of the following statements is true?

   A. The voltage available at the lamps will be 12.6 volts.

   B. The voltage available at the lamps will be 0.0 volts.

   C. The rheostat is working normally.

   D. More information is needed in order to determine whether the lamps will operate correctly.   (E.1.10)

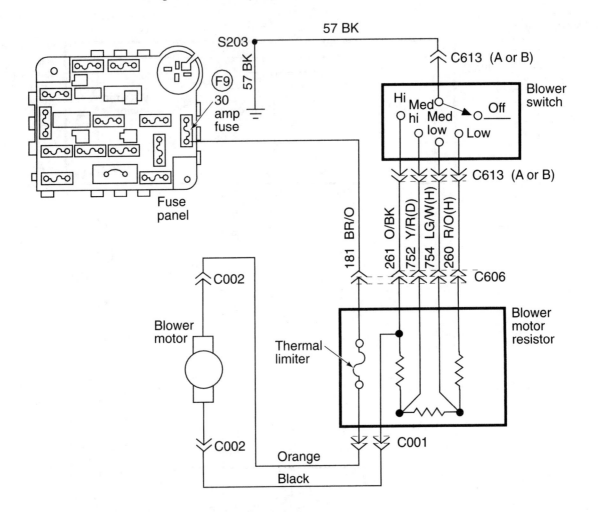

89. The medium-hi speed of the blower motor circuit in the figure shown is inoperative; the rest of the blower speeds are fine. Technician A says circuit 752 may be open. Technician B says the middle resistor in the blower motor resistor assembly may be open. Who is right?

   A. Technician A

   B. Technician B

   C. Both A and B

   D. Neither A nor B   (A.11)

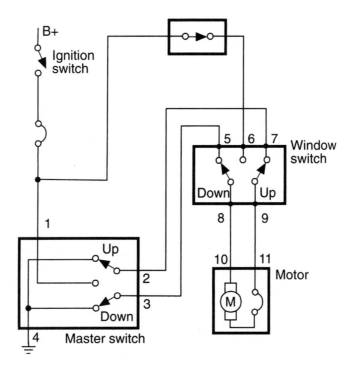

90. The power window motor in the figure shown is completely inoperative. With the master window switch placed in the "down" position, the following voltages are measured at each terminal:

Terminal #	Voltage
1	12V
2	0V
3	12V
4	0V
5	12V
6	12V
7	0V
8	12V
9	0V
10	12V
11	0V

Which of the following statements represents the cause of this problem?

A. The master switch is faulty.

B. The window switch is faulty.

C. The motor is faulty.

D. There is a poor ground in the circuit.   (H.1.2)

Appendices

Answers to the Test Questions for the Sample Test Section 5

1.	A	24.	B	47.	B	70.	D
2.	D	25.	D	48.	A	71.	A
3.	C	26.	A	49.	C	72.	C
4.	D	27.	D	50.	B	73.	D
5.	B	28.	B	51.	C	74.	A
6.	A	29.	B	52.	A	75.	A
7.	A	30.	A	53.	B	76.	B
8.	D	31.	A	54.	D	77.	A
9.	A	32.	A	55.	C	78.	C
10.	A	33.	C	56.	C	79.	D
11.	B	34.	C	57.	A	80.	C
12.	C	35.	C	58.	A	81.	C
13.	A	36.	C	59.	C	82.	D
14.	C	37.	A	60.	C	83.	C
15.	B	38.	B	61.	C	84.	D
16.	A	39.	B	62.	D	85.	B
17.	A	40.	B	63.	A	86.	C
18.	C	41.	B	64.	A	87.	C
19.	D	42.	A	65.	C	88.	B
20.	A	43.	C	66.	B	89.	A
21.	C	44.	B	67.	C	90.	C
22.	B	45.	A	68.	B		
23.	C	46.	C	69.	C		

Explanations to the Test Questions for the Sample Test Section 5

1. With an open circuit there is no current flow; therefore, there are no voltage drops. Full battery voltage would be available in the circuit until the point of the open. In the figure used for this question, the test light is probing the circuit before the open and would illuminate with full power. Any point in the circuit after the open would have no voltage; therefore, the test light would not illuminate. **Answer A is the correct answer.**

2. This is a 12-volt circuit. If the voltage drop across the lamp is 9 volts (as shown), that means 3 volts are being dropped either before the lamp or at the ground of the lamp. Technician A must be wrong; if all else were normal, the voltage drop across the lamp would be 12 volts regardless of the resistance of the light. If the circuit were grounded as suggested by Technician B, there should still be 12 volts across the light. Since A and B are wrong, choice C is also wrong. Therefore **D is the correct answer.**

3. Lower amperage is always caused by higher than normal resistance somewhere in the circuit. Therefore **choice C is correct.** An open circuit has no current flow and therefore A is not correct. A short would cause higher than normal current flow; choice B is also not correct. A blown fuse is caused by a short and, like answers A and B, this would not cause lower than normal current flow through the circuit.

4. Most often a motor grounds through the case and through an external wire attached to the case. Therefore if everything were normal, there would be zero resistance between the two points described by Technician A. An internal short in the motor will not affect this reading; therefore Technician A is wrong. Technician B, on the other hand, is checking the resistance of the entire circuit. If a circuit had a total resistance of zero, the circuit would have to be shorted and not okay. Therefore Technician B is also wrong. **The correct answer is D,** neither A nor B.

5. If the open was in the switch, the bulb would illuminate when the jumper wire bypassed the switch, circuit breaker, and fuse (connected from the battery to the bulb); therefore answers A, C, and D are wrong. By the way, there is no circuit breaker in the diagram. With the jumper wire connected from the ground side of the bulb and a good ground, the normal ground circuit is bypassed. This caused the light to illuminate; therefore **B is correct.**

6. A test light will only light when there is voltage present. Plus, when a test light is placed in series within a circuit, it will only light when current flows through it. Technician B suggests there is an open in the circuit. With an open there is no current flow and the test light will not light; therefore Technician B is wrong. If there is a short before the disconnected connector, current will flow. Therefore Technician A has the right idea and is correct. **The correct answer is A.**

7. In order to measure current flow through the tester, the switch must be closed or turned on. Therefore **choice A is correct.** Choice B allows for too much battery drain; on most vehicles the maximum allowable drain is 50 milliamps. One of the potential problems while doing this test is hurrying through it. The actual drain on the battery does not show up immediately, as suggested by answer C. It may not be shown on the meter until several minutes have passed. Since an open door switches dome and courtesy lights on, there will be a drain on the battery when the door is open. This would prevent measuring true parasitic load, as the current drain from the door would increase the measured drain. Therefore choice D is also incorrect.

8. An infinite reading on an ohmmeter indicates there is an open. A good circuit breaker is closed until high current flows through it, and then it opens. Technician A suggests a good circuit breaker is one that is open not closed and is wrong. A good circuit breaker will have zero resistance. Technician B knows that an ohmmeter runs current through the component being tested in order to measure its resistance. However, the amount of current provided by the meter is very low, too low to cause the circuit breaker to trip or open. Technician B is also wrong. Since both are wrong, **the correct answer is D.**

9. **Answer A is correct.** The figure does show the symbol for a diode. The symbol depicts the function of a diode, a device that allows current to flow in one direction. Note the arrow in the symbol.

10. Battery hydrometer tests are becoming more obsolete over time. However, technicians need to know how to do them for the current ASE test. The hydrometer measures the specific gravity of the battery's electrolyte. This measurement gives an indication of the battery's state of charge. The reading is quite simple to take, but it must be adjusted according to temperature. The base temperature for this test is 80°F. When the temperature is below that, 0.004 should be subtracted from the measurement for every ten degrees below 80. Answer A is wrong because at 0 degrees, 0.032 should be subtracted not 0.050. When the temperature is above 80°F, 0.004 for every ten degrees should be added to the measurement. Therefore choice B is also wrong. At 120°F, the measurement should be increased by 0.016. A fully charged battery will have an adjusted reading of 1.265, not 1.225 as suggested by answer D. **Answer C is correct.** A good battery will not have more than a 0.050 specific gravity reading between cells.

11. While conducting a battery load test, the test load is determined by multiplying the cold-cranking amperage rating by 0.5 (50 percent), by multiplying the amp-hour rating by three, or by referring to the specifications given by the manufacturer. Technician A is using the wrong formula to determine the test load. Technician B is looking at the battery's voltage during the load test. A good battery will have 9.6 volts and Technician B is correct. Therefore, **choice B is correct.**

12. Correctly disconnecting the battery on late-model vehicles will not cause any problems to the computer or to the vehicle itself. The only thing that will happen is that items held in memory by the computers and accessories will disappear. **Answer C is correct.** The other answers are invalid as long as the battery is disconnected and reconnected properly. The negative cable should be the first cable to be disconnected and the last one to be reconnected.

13. It is natural for dirt and grease to collect on the top of a battery. If it is allowed to accumulate, the dirt and grease can form a conductive path between the battery terminals, causing battery drain. Also, normal battery gassing will deposit sulfuric acid as the vapors condense. Over a period of time the sulfuric acid will corrode the battery terminals, cable clamps, and holddown fixtures. As the corrosion builds, it adds resistance to the entire electrical system. Technician A and **answer A are correct;** the condition described in the question could cause battery drain. Technician B is incorrect. Based on what we know from the question, the dirt and corrosion are normal. Rather than replace the battery, it should be removed and cleaned.

14. Although fast charging a battery is not the preferred way to charge, sometimes it is necessary. Fast charging requires that the battery be monitored at all times. Never fast charge a battery for longer than two hours. Also, as told by Technician A, never allow the voltage of a 12-volt battery to exceed 15.5 volts. Nor should you ever allow the temperature to rise above 125°F, as Technician B said. Since both technicians are correct, **the correct answer is C.**

15. Whenever jump-starting a vehicle, it is recommended that the accessories in both vehicles be turned off. Technician A suggests they should be on but is wrong. Technician B is relating the correct location for the negative booster cable and is correct. **The correct answer to this question is B.** When jump-starting a vehicle, make sure the vehicles are not touching each other. Turn off the accessories and make sure the parking brake is set in both vehicles. Connect the positive booster cables first. Then connect one end of the negative cable to the booster battery's negative terminal and the other end to an engine ground on the vehicle being boosted. Once the engine of the boosted vehicle starts, disconnect the negative cable from the engine ground. Then disconnect the rest of the cables.

16. When a voltmeter is connected across something, it displays the voltage difference between the two points. Doing what Technician A says will give the difference in voltage between the positive side of the battery and the negative side. The measurement should be at or very close to battery voltage. Connecting the meter as described by Technician B will display the difference between the voltage at the battery post and the battery terminal. Ideally there would be a zero reading here, but if there is corrosion at the terminal the meter will show some voltage. This is the voltage drop across the battery terminal. Therefore **Technician A is correct.**

17. Keep in mind that the slower a motor turns, the more amperage it will draw. Therefore the only answer that is correct is A. Worn bushings will cause the motor to turn slower than normal and will cause high current draw. The other answers suggest high resistance as the problem. High resistance always causes lower than normal current draw. **Answer A is correct.**

18. When a voltmeter is connected across something, it displays the voltage difference between the two points. In the diagram the voltmeter is shown connected from the negative battery post to the ground at the starter. This connection will only measure the voltage drop across the starter's ground circuit. To measure the voltage drop across the positive battery cable, the meter should be connected at the positive battery post and the starter end of the positive cable. To measure the voltage drop across the solenoid windings, the meter must be connected across the windings. The same is true for the solenoid disc and terminals. Only **answer C is correct.**

19. There are a few things that should be noticed in the story. The voltmeter is connected so it can read the voltage drop across the solenoid. The solenoid drops 12 volts. The starter motor is not working and apparently is dropping very little voltage. (The solenoid is dropping near battery voltage.) The solenoid is working, as evident by the click. Therefore the problem seems to be a bad or shorted starter motor. Technician A is wrong because there seems to be very little voltage dropped in the circuit between the battery and the solenoid. Technician B is also wrong. The solenoid is working. Since they both are wrong, **the correct answer is D.**

20. Basically this is a problem where the starter and solenoid are not doing anything. It could be, as suggested in answer D, an open in the starter circuit. A faulty clutch switch (answer B) could cause an open in the circuit, so it could be a cause. And answer C could also be right, as it could cause the same thing. So the **correct answer must be A.** An undercharged battery probably would not allow the headlights to be bright in the first place. Also, if the starter circuit were okay, the lights would get very dim when the ignition was turned to start. This would happen even though the starter and solenoid could not work because of the low voltage.

21. What Technician A suggests is a great idea. This test makes sure the starter you are about to install works. Therefore Technician A is correct. But so is Technician B. Removing the M terminal to the starter's field coils is part of the proper procedure for checking and adjusting the starter drive to flywheel clearance. **The correct answer is C,** both of the technicians.

22. Normally there are other indications for a seized engine being the cause of a no-crank condition. Although Technician A is correct by wanting to verify that the engine is or is not seized by rotating it with a large wrench, this should not be done first. The first thing to do when facing a no-crank situation is to check the battery, just as Technician B said. **Only Technician B is correct.**

23. In order for an alternator to have output, it must be rotating and it must have field current. If there is an open in field circuit, no field voltage will be available and the unit will have zero output. Likewise, if the fuse or fusible link for the field circuit is open, the alternator will have zero output. Therefore both technicians are correct and **C is the correct answer.**

24. An oscilloscope converts electrical signals into a visual image representing voltage changes over a specific period of time. Answers A, C, and D are all correct. An upward movement of the trace does mean that the voltage has increased, and downward movements show a decrease in voltage. If the trace stays flat, the voltage is staying at that level. Because the trace is showing voltage over time, the movement of the trace represents time across the screen of the oscilloscope. Although the cleanness of the connection will ensure good and clean waveforms, the size and clarity of the trace is dependent on the voltage scale and the time reference selected on the scope. Although choice B is a false statement, **the correct answer to this question is B.**

25. Typically a loose or glazed belt will cause decreased output at high speeds. It will not cause an overcharge condition and Technician A is wrong. So is Technician B. If the grounded field wire did full field the alternator, the output should be high. Therefore **the correct answer is D;** neither of the techs is correct.

26. A shorted diode in a generator will typically cause the amperage output to be about one-third less than normal. **Answer A is correct.** A broken brush would probably cause no or zero output, so B is wrong. Since the test in the question was conducted with the system full-fielded, the regulator will not have an effect on the output and C is wrong. If the capacitor in the alternator were faulty, the system's output would be erratic or there would be zero output. D is also wrong.

27. Obviously 16.2 volts from the charging system is too much for a 12-volt battery. Answer A is correct; this high voltage would cause an overcharged battery. B is also correct; the high voltage could cause damage to electronic components. With an overcharged battery, gassing does increase and answer C is also correct. D, however, is wrong. The high system voltage would increase the brilliance of the lights, not decrease it. So **the correct answer is D,** although it is wrong.

28. Since the battery is not capable of holding a charge, one would reason that the charging system would be higher than normal. High output depends on two primary things: the state of charge of the battery and the amount of current to the generator's field windings. Technician A is wrong in saying the output would be lower. Technician B is correct. With the demands of the battery, a higher output is required. In order to provide the higher output, field current will also be high. **The correct answer is B.**

29. What we are looking at here is a 1.4 volt drop between the generator output terminal and the battery. If there were excessive resistance on the ground side of the alternator, the output at the generator would be less. Technician A is wrong and should notice where the output is being measured. One probe is on the output terminal and the other is to the alternator case. If the ground for the alternator were bad, the ground at the case would be bad and the measured output lower. Excessive resistance in the positive side of the circuit could only cause the voltage drop being witnessed here. Technician B is correct and **answer B is correct.**

30. The charge indicator light is on continuously because the charging system is continuously not putting out a charge. An open in the wire or circuit that connects the out of the generator to the battery would prevent the charging system from charging the battery. It would also cause the indicator to be continuously on, as suggested by Technician A. Technician B is wrong. An open in the bulb circuit would not allow it to work. It would be continuously off. **The correct answer is A.**

31. A good diode will always have low resistance when an ohmmeter is connected across it in one direction and high resistance when the leads are reversed. If the meter indicates two infinite readings, the diode is open and is no good. Likewise, if the meter readings are low in both directions, the diode is shorted. The numbers given in answer D are not good examples of actual readings. The 40 ohms is not considered high when checking a diode. The high reading would more likely be 40K ohms. **The correct answer is A.**

32. Most headlight circuits are equipped with self- or automatic-reset circuit breakers. This is what is happening here. The headlights turn on and off at will because the breaker is opening and closing. The tripping of the breaker is probably caused by an intermittent short, just as Technician A said. A high charging rate would not cause the breaker to trip; nor would the lights turn on and off, they would be brighter. So Technician B is wrong. **The correct answer is A.**

33. When replacing a halogen lightbulb, always turn off the headlights and allow the bulbs to cool. Keep moisture away from the bulb, and handle the bulb by its base. Do not scratch or drop the bulb. Coat the terminals with dielectric grease to minimize corrosion. Answers A, B, and D are all correct statements. C is not a correct statement but **C is the correct answer** to the question.

34. A look at the schematic for the question should lead you to the answer to this question. Technician A suggests that the taillights would not work if fuse 14 were blown. Actually, if fuse 12 was blown, the taillights would not work. Technician B suggests the stoplights would not work. This circuit is not part of the circuit in the schematic and therefore would not be affected by fuse 14. The instrument cluster or panel lights would be affected. Fuse 14 is the protection device for that circuit. Therefore **answer C is correct.** By the way, the low beams would still work if fuse 14 were blown because they are in the circuit with fuse 13.

35. The least likely cause of the problem in this question is C, a poor headlamp ground. This problem would affect the brilliance of the headlight, not the performance of the retractable door. The other answers or statements are correct. Electrically operated systems generally incorporate a headlamp control module, which provides power to the headlamp door motors in response to signals received from the headlamp circuit. The movement of the door is halted once in position by a limit switch. Some headlamp door retractors are vacuum operated. Any condition that would cause low vacuum will slow or prevent headlamp door operation. **C is the correct answer** to this question.

36. Daytime running lights (DRL) are typically part of the vehicle's high-beam circuit. The control circuit is connected directly to the vehicle's ignition switch, so the lights are turned on whenever the vehicle is running. The circuit is equipped with a module that reduces battery voltage to approximately 6- volts. This voltage reduction allows the high beams to burn with less intensity and prolongs the life of the bulbs. When the headlight switch is moved to the ON position, the module is deactivated and the lights work normally. Both technicians are correct. Troubleshooting these systems should begin by identifying whether the problem is in the DRL system or the headlight system. If the problem is in the headlight system, service to the circuit and lamps is conducted in the same way as for vehicles that are not equipped with DRL. If the problem is in the DRL system and the headlights work normally, only that part of the circuit that is unique to the DRL can be the problem. **The correct answer is C.**

37. Technician A is correct. When checking dim taillight problems, determine if only one or all of the taillights are dim. If all of the taillights are dim, then there is a high resistance between the headlight switch and the common point to all the taillights. If only one taillight is dim, then there is a bad ground between the common point and the individual taillight. Most likely the taillight or the surrounding metal has corroded at the point where the taillight is grounded. Technician B's suggestion would affect all of the taillights. **The correct answer is A**.

38. This is an interesting wiring diagram and one that will try your patience tracing through the wires. Upon examination you will notice the grounds for the lights are redundant. So if one of the grounds is bad, the lights will still function normally. Only **answer B is correct.** The other answers assume the loss of a ground for the circuit.

39. Technician B is correct and shows an understanding of typical instrument cluster illumination circuits. Bulbs in the instrument cluster are connected in parallel, so that if one bulb were to fail, the rest of the bulbs would still be able to illuminate. The rheostat is connected in series with the instrument cluster bulbs. When the rheostat control knob is rotated, the voltage to the instrument cluster bulbs is reduced. This action lowers the current flow and reduces the brilliance of the bulbs. If the rheostat circuit were open, no current would be at the bulbs. **The correct answer is B.**

40. Answer A presents a problem that would affect only one bulb, not all of the bulbs, and is therefore a wrong answer. Both C and D suggest a problem that would not tend to be intermittent. Both of these problems would cause the bulbs to be off continuously. **Answer B is correct.** When diagnosing an instrument cluster for intermittent problems, check the common ground for all the bulbs. If there is no common ground, inspect the printed circuit for cracks where the power comes in from the headlight switch. A loose wire or connection at any common point will cause this intermittent failure.

41. None of the courtesy lights work. The problem must be in that part of the circuit that affects the entire circuit. Of the answer choices only answer B would affect all of the courtesy lights. In an insulated side door jamb switch system, the door jamb switches are connected between the battery positive terminal and the courtesy lightbulbs. A separate ground wire is connected to the other side of each bulb. An open circuit to one door jamb switch would only affect the operation of the courtesy lights when that door was opened. If a short to ground should occur at the door jamb switch, then that courtesy light circuit would fail. **The correct answer is B.**

42. By looking at the wiring diagram, you will notice that circuit 156 is the controlled ground circuit. The switches that control the courtesy lights normally provide a ground. If this circuit was grounded at the mentioned splice, the circuit would operate independently of the switches and the courtesy lights would stay on at all times. **The correct answer is A.** Obviously this is the opposite of what answer B says, and that answer choice is wrong. Circuit 156 has nothing to with the under-hood light, so that light would be unaffected by the short. Therefore choice C is wrong. D is also wrong, as the short is not on the power side of the circuit. If it were, the fuse would blow.

43. Instrument panel or cluster light circuits are activated when the headlights are turned on. A separate rheostat is used to control the brightness of the lamps. Power typically is provided to the lamps from the headlight switch through the rheostat. Technician A is correct. The printed circuit mounted to the back of the instrument cluster contains the electrical pathways for the instruments and the lamps. If a printed circuit board is damaged or has a fault, it must be replaced and cannot be repaired. Technician B is also correct. Since both technicians are correct, **the correct answer is C.**

44. Three of the answers (A, C, and D) correctly state conditions that would cause premature composite bulb failure. A high charging rate will cause the bulbs to burn brighter and hotter than normal, leading to premature failure. If a composite bulb is handled improperly, such as the presence of skin oil or grease on the bulb's glass envelope, it will prematurely burn out. Likewise and for the same reasons, dirt, rain, mud, and so on, can contaminant the bulb as the debris enters through a crack in the lamp cover or housing. **The correct answer to the question is B.** Excessive resistance in the bulb's ground circuit would cause it to burn less bright and generate less heat, thereby extending its useful life.

45. The signal light flasher contains a bimetallic contact arm that is surrounded by a heating coil. There is one contact on the bimetallic arm and another that is stationary. When the ignition is on, voltage is supplied through the flasher contacts to the turn signal switch. This switch directs the voltage to either the left or right turn signal circuits in response to turn signal switch position selected by the driver. When current starts to flow through the flasher unit, the heating coil warms the bimetallic arm, which then bends and separates the contacts. With the contact open, the heating coil and bimetallic arm cool and allow the contact to close. This opening and closing of the contact is repeated to provide the flashing action of the circuit. If resistance in the circuit is increased, the current flow through the circuit will be reduced. This would lengthen the heat/cool cycle of the bimetallic contact. As Technician A says, the result will be a slower flashing rate. A bulb with higher wattage will draw more current than normal because its resistance is decreased. The increase in current will heat the heating element faster and therefore decrease the heat/cool cycle of the bimetallic contact arm. The result is a faster flash rate. Technician B is wrong, so **the correct answer is A.**

46. To correctly answer this question you need to trace three different wires and apply different potential problems to each, then figure out what would happen. After you have done that, match what you know would happen to the answer choices. Answer A relates to high resistance in wire DB 180G RD. This wire belongs to the left signal circuit and would not affect the right side. It would cause dim and/or slow operation of the left side signals. The problem in choice B is a short to ground in the same circuit. Again, only the left side would be affected. High resistance in wire D7 18BR RD (answer C) would affect the operation of the right side. Choice D is also a high resistance problem, but the chosen wire is common to all of the turn signals and therefore would not have an effect on just one side. **The correct answer is C.**

47. The backup lights do not work at all. This is a good indication of an open circuit. The presence of 12 volts at both sides of the bulb indicates the open is after the bulbs. The only thing after the bulbs is the ground. That must be where the open is. In fact, an open here explains why 12 volts was measured on both sides of the bulb: the circuit is incomplete and has no ground. When there is no ground, there is no current flow. Without current there will be no voltage drop across the bulbs. **Answer B is correct.** The other answer choices would not cause the bulbs not to work; they would affect the operation, but the bulbs would still work.

48. A short to ground always increases circuit current flow if the short is on the power side of the circuit. The increase in current can cause the circuit's fuse to blow, just like Technician A said. However, the short would affect the entire circuit, not just the side it is in. Therefore Technician B is wrong. **The correct answer is A.**

49. The gauge in the figure for this question is a thermal-electric gauge. These gauges contain a bimetallic strip surrounded by a heating coil. The pivoted gauge pointer is connected to the bimetallic strip. The sending unit contains a variable resistor. In a fuel gauge, this variable resistor is connected to a float in the fuel tank. If the tank is filled with fuel, the sending unit resistance decreases, and the current flow through the bimetallic strip increases. This increased current flow heats the bimetallic strip and pushes the pointer toward the full position. A short to ground in the circuit between the sending unit and the gauge would also increase current and force the gauge to always read full, which is what answer C says. High resistance in the sending unit ground wire would cause the gauge to read too low at all times. Therefore choice A is wrong. The same would result from the presence of high resistance between the IVR and the gauge, so B is also wrong. Anytime there is an open, if there was an open as described in choice D, the gauge would not work. **The correct answer is C.**

50. **The correct answer is B.** Technician B correctly identified the IVR as a possible cause of the problem. A defective voltage limiter may also cause low or erratic readings on all the gauges. Since the purpose of the IVR is to supply a steady voltage to the gauges, when it is faulty the gauges will receive erratic or low voltages. Technician A suspected that the alternator is to blame for the condition. When functioning properly, the IVR supplies about 5V to the gauges regardless of the charging system voltage.

51. The problem stated in this question is that some of the segments of the fuel gauge in a digital instrument cluster are not illuminating. The question asked for the way to fix the problem. Answer A is wrong because individual segments cannot be repaired or replaced. Answer B says the problem may be in the fuel gauge circuit. This cannot be right, because some of the segments work and others do not. If the circuit were bad, erroneous gauge readings would result. Another problem, answer D, blames the problem on the IVR. Again, if this were bad, we would have erratic or low readings on the gauges. **C is the correct answer.** The only way to fix the problem of the missing gauge segments is to replace the entire instrument cluster.

52. Regardless of the system, a digital speedometer depends on the input from a speed sensor to display the speed of the vehicle. If the sensor is faulty, as suggested by Technician A, the speedometer may not receive any speed inputs and the gauge will read zero. Technician B knows that the computer controls rely heavily on the throttle position sensor but fails to realize that the TP sensor is not used to determine speed. It is used as an input to the computer so that it can compare throttle opening with speed and help determine vehicle load and operating conditions. **A is the correct answer.**

53. Warning lights are simple circuits. Power is supplied to the light at all times, and the sending unit switches to open or close the circuit by completing the path to ground. When satisfactory conditions are met, the circuit is open and the bulb is off. Any problem that opens the circuit will keep the light off at all times. Answers A, C, and D all suggest an open circuit and would cause the problem. Answer B will not cause the problem; if anything, it would cause the light to illuminate constantly. **B is the correct answer.**

54. Anytime a system works intermittently, suspect a loose or bad connection. This is probably the cause of the problem in this question. The cause cited by Technician A, an open in the circuit to the warning chime, would cause the chime never to sound. If the switch circuit were shorted to ground, as suggested by Technician B, the chime would never stop. **The correct answer is D;** neither of the techs is correct.

55. This problem would really be annoying to the customer, especially that buzzer. If you look at the wiring diagram given with the question, you will notice that the buzzer and light are designed to stay on for some time even if the seat belt is fastened. They will also continue if the belt is not fastened. There are two basic control switches: the timer contacts and the seat belt switch. Both work independently of each other. The cause of constant operation would have to be something that keeps the contacts of both the timer and the switch closed. What that something is we do not know, but of all the answer choices given for this question, only **C is correct.** The other choices would not cause the buzzer and light to stay on.

56. Technician A is correct. If the tone generator does not work at all, the sounding device is bad or there is an open in the circuit. If the generator works constantly, the existence of the situation the device was designed to warn the driver about or the controlling circuit is shorted and the switch or sender bypassed. If the audible warning is heard intermittently, the most likely cause is a loose wire or connector. Technician B says the tone generator should be checked for operation by running it through the prescribed self-test mode. This is also correct. Many of the warning systems on today's vehicles are triggered by a PCM or BCM. Always refer to the testing methods recommended by the manufacturer when testing these systems. **The correct answer is C,** because both technicians are correct.

57. In the horn circuit given for the question, the horn is activated by depressing the horn switch that completes the relay circuit to ground. The relay is then activated and the horn sounds. If the horn sounds continuously, something is providing a ground for the relay or the relay contacts are stuck closed. Technician A correctly diagnosed the problem by saying the wire from the relay to switch must be grounded. This problem would bypass the horn button. If the relay points were stuck in an open position, the horn would never work. Technician B is wrong. **The correct answer is A.**

58. Most horn circuits are controlled by relays. When the horn button is depressed, the ground for the relay's coil is provided. This closes the circuit and a small flow of electrical current through the coil energizes the electromagnet that pulls on a moveable arm. The electrical contacts on the arm complete the circuit from the battery to the horn causing the horn to sound. The most likely cause for both horns not working at all is that the horns are bad or there is an open in the part of the circuit that is common to both horns. This is the case for all of the answers but A. If the open were only in the circuit for the left horn, the right horn would work fine. **The correct answer is A.**

59. Both technicians are correct. The possible causes for low-speed only operation are a faulty wiper switch, worn brushes, poor circuit connections, or an open in the control circuit. Many motors are equipped with three brushes riding on the armature. Two are located directly opposite of each other and are used for all speeds. The third brush is used for high-speed operation only. **The correct answer is C.**

60. In many vehicles equipped with intermittent or interval wiper motor circuits a variable resistor in the intermittent wiper control module provides a voltage input to the intermittent wiper module. This module operates the wiper motor to provide the proper delay. If the variable resistor is faulty, the feed to the wiper motor will not correctly control the motor. Technician A is correct. On some vehicles, the intermittent wiper function is incorporated into the BCM. These systems may have a self-diagnostic mode that looks at the wiper circuit. Like all electronic components, do not attempt to measure the resistance of the module or the variable resistor unless instructed to do so by the manufacturer. Technician B is also correct. **The correct answer is C.**

61. Slow moving or dimly operating electrical parts are typically caused by excessive resistance. The increased circuit resistance decreases the current through the circuit causing the motor to run slowly or a bulb to burn dimmer. This is the logic used by Technician B, who is correct. However, when we have a motor that is performing some mechanical function, there is a possibility that mechanical things are preventing the motor from turning at its normal speed. This is what Technician A suggests and he is also correct. To determine which of these is the cause of the problem, you can measure the current flow in the circuit. If the problem is excessive electrical resistance, the circuit's current will be low. If the problem is mechanical, the current will be higher than normal due to the slow rotating motor. **The correct answer is C.**

62. Because the windshield wipers function normally, you can assume that the fuse for the circuit is okay. It is unlikely that the vehicle will have a separate fuse for the washer system; therefore answer D is not a likely cause of the problem. The other answer choices are likely causes. When diagnosing a wind-shield washer system, begin by checking for low fluid levels and disconnected wires. Then try to isolate the problem by disconnecting the hose at the pump and operating the system. If the pump ejects a stream of fluid, then the hoses are clogged. If the pump does not spray, observe the pump motor while activating the washer switch. If the motor operates, check for blockage at the pump. If there is no blockage, replace the motor. If the motor fails to operate, check for voltage and ground at the motor. This will isolate the problem to the motor or the washer switch and wires. **The correct answer is D.**

63. Whenever there is an intermittent type problem, always suspect that something is loose or poorly connected. In this question only Technician A uses that logic. A loose ground could cause an inter-mittent failure and could, if it were very loose, not allow the pump to work at all. Technician B's suspicion that there is an open would be another explanation for the pump not working, but an open would not cause an intermittent problem. This assumes the open stays an open and is not the result of a loose wire. **The correct answer is A.**

64. Because the windows work normally through the master switch, we know the motors and their related circuits are fine. As we look over the diagram to identify the parts of the circuit for the win-dow switch, we find that A is the best answer from the list of answer choices. If there is an open between the ignition switch and the window switch, the window switch cannot send voltage to the motor and the window will not work. Since the window switch circuit is separate from the master switch circuit, the window would operate through the master switch in spite of the problem. If there were an open in the window switch, the master switch would not move the window either. An open in the master switch ground wire would also make the window inoperative from the mas-ter switch. If there were a short to ground at the motor's circuit breaker, the window would not operate properly from either switch. **The correct answer is A.**

65. The window does not move when activated by the window switch. We know parts of the circuit are good because the LR window works normally. Diagnosis should begin by determining what type of electrical problem we have. Since the window does not work, an open is the most likely problem. Both technicians have identified this as the basic problem. Now if we look at the wiring diagram and note where the techs describe the open and then determine what the effect would be, we will be able to see which tech is right. They both are. An open between the RR window switch and ground would remove the ground from the motor and it will not be able to work. If the contacts at the RR window switch are stuck or remain open, the motor will never be activated. Therefore, **the correct answer is C.**

66. The question asks what item in the list could not be the cause for two different types of problems: slow operation and no operation. All of the items would appear as a possible cause for both prob-lems except a faulty switch. If the switch were bad, slow operation would not be possible as the seat would not move unless the circuit to a motor was complete. It is the job of the switch to close the circuit. **The correct answer is B** because it would not be a likely cause for both problems.

67. This is another except-type question. The only answer choice that would not affect horizontal move-ment is C. An open in the switch to ground circuit would affect the total operation of the seat. A jammed seat track, an open between the switch and the horizontal motor, and burned contact in the horizontal seat switch would all hinder or prevent horizontal movement. **The correct answer is C.**

68. Rear window defoggers are simply a parallel circuit of resistor wires spread across or laminated into the rear glass. The voltage drop across these wires generates heat that clears the window. When the rear defogger switch is pressed, a signal is sent to a solid-state timer. When this signal is received, the timer grounds the relay winding. Under this condition, the relay supplies battery voltage to the defogger grid. After a preset time, the timer opens the relay, shutting off the grid current. All of the statements in the question are true except for B, which incorrectly states the amount of voltage sup-plied to the grid. Therefore **the correct answer is B.**

69. Answer A says the voltage drop from the groundside of the grid to an engine ground should not exceed one volt. This is not true. Battery voltage should be dropped by the grid and zero volts dropped at the ground. If there is a voltage drop at the ground, we have a bad ground. Choice B says a 12-volt test light should be illuminated at half brilliance at any place on the grid. This is false. The brilliance of the test light should decrease as it moves from the positive side to the negative, simply because voltage is being dropped along the grid. Choice C states the test light will not illuminate on part of a grid if there is an open. This is true. Another indication of an open grid (besides the fact that the window will not be cleared around that grid) is that the test light will have full brilliance before the open. After the open, the test light will not come on. Between the two is the location of the open. Answer D says the opposite of what to expect. The brilliance of the test light decreases as it moves toward the negative or ground side of the grid. **The correct answer is C.**

70. The key to answering this question is to note that the unlock and lock functions are separate. There are two controlling circuits: one for lock and one for unlock. The problem in this question is that the locks do not work, not that they do not lock or do not unlock. Technician A describes a probable cause for the locks not locking. Technician B does the same for the locks not unlocking. So neither is correct. The problem lies in the circuit where it is common to both functions, such as the fuse. **The correct answer is D.**

71. The cause of all of the locks not working in the lock mode must be somewhere in the circuit that is common to all of the doors. The cause could be the inability to disable the unlock mode or something that prevents the lock mode from being activated. Answer A is correct because an open ground at the unlock relay contacts would cause this problem. The lock motors get their ground through that connection. Choice B would only affect one lock and therefore is not a possible cause for the problem in the question. Answer C suggests an open in the circuit between the master switch and the lock relay coil. This may prevent master switch operation but not the door switch operation. Answer D would only affect the individual door lock switches and not the master. Therefore, **answer A is correct.**

72. Sometimes there are easy questions on the test and this is one of them. Remote keyless entry systems use a transmitter that is battery powered to lock and unlock the doors, as well as other functions. The remote keyless entry module is connected to the power door lock circuit. A small remote transmitter sends lock and unlock signals to this module when the appropriate buttons are pressed on the remote transmitter. When the unlock button is pressed on the remote transmitter, the module supplies voltage to the unlock relay winding to close these relay contacts and move the door lock motors to the unlock position. When the unlock button is depressed on the remote transmitter, the locks will unlock and the interior lights will illuminate on most systems. Then the remote keyless entry module will turn off the interior lights after approximately one minute, or when the ignition is turned on. **The correct answer is C.**

73. **Choice D is the correct answer** because it is actually wrong. Most remote control units need to be fairly close to activate or deactivate the door locks; 100 yards is quite far away. The other statements are true. The interior lights are normally energized with the unlock function. These lights also are typically set to a timer that causes them to turn off after a short period of time, perhaps a minute later. Also, the systems are designed to turn off the lights once the ignition is turned on or very shortly afterwards.

74. The most likely cause for an inoperative sunroof listed in this question is choice A. If there were an open in the power saver relay winding, the relay would never energize and the power to both the open and close relay windings would not be present. The sunroof would not move. Choice B suggests an open in close relay winding, C suggests an open in close relay, and D offers an open in the close relay and switch. All of these would only affect the close mode of operation. Although they are correct for that mode, they are not probable causes for all modes of operation. **The correct answer is A.**

75. The major cause of a fuse blowing is a short; therefore, it is highly likely that the cause of the problem is a short in the fuse's circuit. Fuse 17 is the true fuse for this sunroof circuit. If the power saver relay winding is shorted to ground, the fuse will blow. Therefore Technician A is correct. If the short is between the power saver relay winding and ground, all we have is a redundant ground and the fuse will not blow. Technician B is incorrect. **The correct answer is A.**

76. In the diagram you will notice that voltage is supplied through a fuse to the power mirror switch assembly. When the mirror select switch is in the left position, it supplies voltage to the left mirror motor. When the left/right switch is pressed to the left position, a ground connection is completed from the left/right motor through the switch to the ground. Under this condition, the motor moves the left side mirror to the left. Similar action happens for all other directions and the right side mirror. There is only one true statement in the answer choices, B. Therefore, **the correct answer is B.**

77. On vehicles with heated rear view mirrors, the heating element in the mirror is activated when the rear defogger button is pressed. Once it is activated, a timer relay supplies voltage to the rear defogger grid and also to the heated mirror element. After a preset period of time, the timer relay shuts off the voltage supply to the defogger grid and the heated mirror element. Turning off the heated mirror is done automatically and does not rely on input from the driver, who undoubtedly will have forgotten it was turned on. Technician B is not correct. **The correct answer is A.**

78. Static may be caused by the charging system or the ignition system. A poor engine ground or poor ground at the sound system components may cause static in the sound. Defective radio suppression devices, such as a suppression coil on an instrument voltage limiter or a clamping diode on an electromagnetic clutch, may cause static on the radio. A defective antenna with poor ground shielding may also result in static. As you can see, both technicians pointed to probable causes for static. **The correct answer is C.**

79. All of the statements are true, except D, which states there should be continuity between the end of the antenna mast and the antenna mounting hardware. If this were to happen, the entire vehicle would try to become the antenna and the result would be poor reception and static. When testing an antenna with an ohmmeter, continuity should be present between the end of the antenna mast and the center pin on the lead-in wire. Continuity also should be present between the ground shell on the lead-in wire and the antenna mounting hardware. No continuity should exist between the center pin on the lead-in wire and the ground shell. **The correct answer is D** because it is not a true statement.

80. To answer this question, think about what is happening in this power antenna circuit. When the radio is turned on, voltage is supplied to the relay winding. This action moves the relay points to the up position, and current flows through the motor to move the antenna upward. When the antenna is fully extended, the up limit switch opens and stops the current flow through the motor. When the radio is turned off, current flow through the relay coil stops. Under this condition, the relay contacts move to the down position. This action reverses current flow through the motor and moves the antenna downward. When the antenna is fully retracted, the down limit switch opens and stops the current flow through the motor. Of the answer choices, only the down limit switch could cause the problem. If the down limit switch is open, the motor will never be activated to bring the antenna down. **The correct answer is C.** The other answers would affect the total operation of the antenna.

81. Technician A is correct by beginning the troubleshooting by looking at the brake light switch. This switch cancels the cruise control function, and if it is defective, cruise control may not be able to activate. Technician B is also correct. Before moving into more detailed electrical diagnosis, make sure the throttle and cruise control linkages are properly connected. After this, and still before electrical checks, make sure the vacuum line and servo are in good shape. **The correct answer is C** because both of the techs are correct.

82. All of the answer choices in this question are true with the exception of D, an open field winding. This problem would tend to decrease the chance of radio noise because the alternator (a major source of noise) would not work. If the stator, a diode in the alternator, or a noise suppression capacitor were defective, these could be the source of the noise. A defective alternator will usually cause a whining noise. **The correct answer is D.**

83. Again, sometimes there are easy questions. To answer this, think about what could cause a fuse to blow. The obvious answer is high current flow, which results from a short. Of the answer choices only C suggests a short and therefore can be the only cause of the problem. D comes close, but this is a short on the ground side and it will not affect current flow. The short just becomes a redundant ground. The other answers focus on high resistance. High resistance always decreases current flow, and low current will never cause a fuse to blow. **The correct answer is C.**

84. All of the answer choices would cause the problem except D. If wire B/R were grounded at the clock connector, the display light would have a ground and its operation would not be controlled by the illumination control. It would be full bright at all times, but the clock would still work. The other answer choices would stop the clock from working. **The correct answer is D.**

85. On vehicles with an electronic cruise control, a control module and stepper motor are combined in one unit. A cable is connected from the stepper motor to the throttle linkage. The control unit receives inputs from the cruise control switch, brake switch, and VSS. The control module sends output commands to the stepper motor to provide the desired throttle opening. If a cruise control cable adjustment is required on these systems, remove the cruise control cable from the throttle linkage. With the throttle closed and the cable pulled all the way outward, install the cable on the throttle linkage. Turn the adjuster screw on the cruise control cable to obtain a 0.0197 in (5 mm) lash in the cable. Only **choice B is correct.** The other choices relate to sensors that are not part of the cruise control circuit. This is especially true of D, because these systems do not rely on the speedometer cable. They rely on the VSS.

86. I will tell you right now, both techs are correct. If the system does not disarm on the driver's side, move to the other side. If the system now disarms, the problem is in the driver's lock mechanism or circuit. One of the most difficult things about diagnosing an anti-theft system is that the circuits and wires are hidden. If they were not, someone could easily get around the system and defeat the purpose for having the system. The only way to identify the circuit and its components is by studying the wiring diagram and by using a component locator guide. **The correct answer is C.**

87. **The correct answer is C.** If the door ajar switches are corroded or damaged, they cannot complete the circuit telling the anti-theft controller that the doors are open. Likewise, most vehicles have circuits that turn on the interior lights when a door is opened. If the lights do not come on when the door is opened, you know the switch is bad.

88. The only systems that are equipped with a siren (choice B) are aftermarket systems. Most factory-installed systems will sound the vehicle's horn(s) and disable the starter if it detects an attempt to break into one of its coverage zones. **The correct answer is B.**

89. The air bag warning light is designed to illuminate whenever the system detects a fault in the system. The light does not come on when the bag deploys. The driver and passenger will notice if the bag deploys and there is no need for a warning light. Only Technician A is correct in this case and **A is the correct answer.** In most air bag systems, the warning light is illuminated for five to six seconds after the engine is started while the module performs system checks. The air bag warning light will then turn off if the system passes all its system tests. If the warning light stays illuminated, then there is a fault with the air bag system.

90. When servicing the air bag system, always disconnect the battery negative terminal first and wait for the manufacturer's specified time period to elapse. This time period is usually one or two minutes. Never use a powered test light to diagnose an air bag system. Diagnose these systems with a voltmeter or the manufacturer's recommended diagnostic tool(s). Use of an ohmmeter should be restricted to circuits without connections to pyrotechnic devices. Since deployed air bags may contain residual chemicals, wear safety glasses and gloves when handling these components. Always store inflator modules faceup on the bench, and carry these components with the trim cover facing away from your body. **The correct answer is C;** never use a test light to check the system.

Answers to the Test Questions for the Additional Test Questions Section 6

1.	C	24.	D	47.	B	70.	A
2.	B	25.	B	48.	C	71.	B
3.	C	26.	B	49.	C	72.	D
4.	D	27.	B	50.	D	73.	C
5.	B	28.	A	51.	A	74.	B
6.	A	29.	C	52.	C	75.	C
7.	A	30.	C	53.	C	76.	B
8.	C	31.	C	54.	A	77.	A
9.	D	32.	D	55.	B	78.	C
10.	D	33.	B	56.	B	79.	A
11.	B	34.	C	57.	B	80.	D
12.	B	35.	A	58.	C	81.	D
13.	A	36.	C	59.	C	82.	B
14.	C	37.	D	60.	C	83.	B
15.	C	38.	A	61.	A	84.	A
16.	A	39.	A	62.	D	85.	B
17.	C	40.	D	63.	B	86.	B
18.	B	41.	B	64.	C	87.	D
19.	D	42.	C	65.	A	88.	B
20.	B	43.	C	66.	B	89.	A
21.	A	44.	B	67.	D	90.	C
22.	B	45.	A	68.	D		
23.	B	46.	C	69.	B		

Explanations to the Test Questions for the Additional Test Questions Section 6

1. **C is the correct answer** because 12 volts should be available before the horn.

2. This is a simple Ohm's law problem. Since all of the resistors are in series, the answer is 12 ohms. **The correct answer is B.**

3. A short always causes higher than normal current flow, except when it is after all loads in the circuit. So Technician A is correct. Whenever there is resistance and current flow in a circuit, voltage is dropped across the resistance. Therefore Technician B is correct in saying that higher resistance in a winding will cause a higher than normal voltage drop across the winding. **Answer C is correct.**

4. When an ohmmeter is connected to a circuit breaker, the meter should read zero ohms if the component is working properly. An open circuit breaker, fuse, or fuse link causes an infinite ohmmeter reading. Never connect an ohmmeter to a powered circuit because meter damage can occur. Both techs are wrong so **the correct answer is D.**

5. **The correct answer to this question is B.** If you had problems, refer to the Overview Section of this guide and study the symbols shown there. Also look in a good textbook or service manual for more electrical schematic symbols.

6. This question contains a summary of all of the bulb circuits mentioned in the question. **The correct answer is A.** Typically the turn signal and brake lights share a common bulb filament. Answer C suggests that the taillights and stoplight share a filament. This is not true; the brake lights operate brighter than the taillights. Answer B is wrong because backup lamps normally have a single filament. Choice D is wrong because the brake pedal switch closes the circuit when the pedal is depressed.

7. The clue to answering this question is to think about what is happening. A normal light bulb in a normal circuit will only burn brighter if more voltage is applied to it. This is exactly what A says. Higher charging system voltage will cause the bulb to be brighter. B is wrong because high resistance in the circuit would cause the lights to be dimmer. C is also wrong because a shorted diode would decrease the output of the charging system and would probably result in a somewhat dimmer bulb. The same is true for high resistance in the battery wire from an alternator, so D is also wrong. **The correct answer is A.**

8. Anytime a fuse blows, suspect a short in the affected circuit. Answer A refers to a short, but it is in the stoplight circuit, so it is unlikely that this would cause the taillight fuse to blow. Choice B is an open and opens do not blow fuses. Choice C is an intermittent short to ground in the taillight wire; this would definitely blow the fuse whenever the wire contacts ground. Answer D would cause intermittent failure of the lights but would not cause the fuse to blow because it is not a short, it would be an open. **The correct answer is C.**

9. **The correct answer is D.** Choice A is wrong because a wire shorted to ground between the turn signal light switch and the left front signal light would likely blow the fuse and neither turn signals would work. Choice B is also wrong. High resistance between the LF signal and ground would also affect hazard light operation, which work properly. The correct answer cannot be C because both techs are wrong.

10. The problem in question is simply that there is no voltage being applied to the backup lamps. The only possible cause listed in the answers is an open wire between the switch and the lamps. If the filaments were shorted, there would be 12 volts available at the bulbs. Also, it is very unlikely that both bulbs would have the same problem. If there were an open between one bulb and ground, only that one bulb would be affected. High resistance in a bulb circuit would cause dim operation. Considering all of these facts, answers A, B, and C are wrong. **The correct answer is D.**

11. While answering this question, it may be easier to identify the least likely causes, then figure out the most likely. Choice D is very unlikely because high resistance will not stop something from working unless it is so bad that it acts like an open. An open will stop something from working. But an open in the lockout switch will affect only the individual window switch. Therefore A is wrong. Choice C would have the same effect and would be wrong. **The correct answer is B.**

12. The key to this question is the phrase "without touching the seat control buttons." Technician A would be correct if the circuit opened while the seat was being moved. Whatever was jamming the seat could give enough physical resistance to slow the motor down and cause the breaker to break. But the problem happens when the seat is not moving. Technician B might be right. If there is a short in the power side of the circuit, that short will trip the breaker regardless of seat movement. Because the breakers are typically self-resetting, the circuit opens and closes. **The correct answer is B.**

13. Because the problem affects only the left side, the problem must be in the circuit that controls the left side. The possible cause given by Technician A is in that part of the circuit and is a likely cause. The cause given by Technician B, however, also affects the operation of the right side. Since the right side works okay, **the correct answer is A.**

14. The top goes down but does not go up. This could be a real problem if the sky opens up and it starts to rain. This is one of those systems that uses electric circuits to move mechanical linkages. Therefore both need to be considered as the cause of the problem and both need to be checked. On the electrical side of things, diagnosis should be focused on the "up" side of the circuit. Answer A must be wrong since the motor and circuit works to take the top down. Choice B is wrong because an open ground wire at the switch would stop the top from going up or down. Choice C relates to the linkage. Since moving the top requires more strain on the system, it is very likely that a binding linkage will be more noticeable when the top is moving up rather than down. So answer choice C is a likely cause of the problem. Choice D suggests a problem that does not allow the top to move up or down. **The correct answer is C.**

15. The basic problem here is a battery that is not receiving enough charge from the charging system. We can assume the problem is not the battery because the question makes no mention of needing to jump-start or recharge the battery. The problem is just that the battery is not receiving enough charge. But the battery is receiving enough charge to keep the indicator lamp off. Choice A suggests a high charging rate due to a faulty voltage regulator. This cannot be right. Constant overcharging can cause battery damage, but the battery is fine. Answer B suggests an open generator field circuit that would cause a dead battery, not just an undercharged battery. Also, the charge indicator lamp would glow. Choice D suggests worn alternator brushes, which would drastically reduce alternator output and certainly would light the indicator lamp. The only possible cause of this problem is C, a shorted diode. **The correct answer is C.**

16. As is the case with any abnormally high resistance, unwanted voltage drops occur across the resistance. This is what Technician A suggests and he is right. The resistance in the alternator to battery circuit will decrease the amount of charge the battery receives. As a result, the battery may be undercharged. It is very unlikely that Technician B is correct. Since high resistance also reduces current flow, it is not very probable that the high resistance described in the question would cause damage to the regulator. If the opposite were true and there was high current, then the regulator could be damaged. **The correct answer is A.**

17. Static may be caused by the charging system or the ignition system. A poor engine ground or poor ground at the sound system components may cause static in the sound. Static can also result from poor grounds at the hood and other body components since they tend to help shield the RFI of the engine from the radio. Defective radio suppression devices, such as a suppression coil on an instrument voltage limiter or a clamping diode on an electromagnetic clutch, may cause static on the radio. A defective antenna with poor ground shielding may also result in static. Both technicians are correct and **the correct answer is C.**

18. Alternator noise when heard on a vehicle's radio tends to be a steady hum that increases as engine speed increases. The noise in this question is not a hum, it is a snap. Technician A is wrong. The noise does, however, increase with an increase in engine speed, so it does have something to do with the engine. In fact, Technician B probably has identified the most likely cause of the problem: something related to the ignition system, such as a loose or defective spark plug wire. By the way, when the voltage in a plug wire escapes and contacts an engine ground, it does make a snapping noise. **The correct answer is B.**

19. Both technicians are wrong. Today's digital clock has very little power consumption, so there is no need to disconnect the clock for any reason. It would take many years for a clock to drain a battery. **The correct answer is D.**

20. Some gauges contain two coils, and the pointer is mounted on a magnet under these coils. In a temperature gauge, the sending unit is connected to the hot coil and the cold coil is grounded. If the coolant is cold, the sending unit has a high resistance. Under this condition, current flows through the lower resistance of the cold coil. Coil magnetism around the cold coil attracts the magnet and the pointer to the cold position. As the coolant temperature increases, the sending unit resistance decreases. When the engine is at normal operating temperature, the current flows through the lower resistance of the hot coil and sending unit. This action attracts the magnet and the pointer to the hot position. When the gauge reads low, the problem could be a low magnetic field around the hot coil. Technician A suggests that low readings could result from a short to ground in the wire between the sending unit and the gauge. If there were a short here, the gauge would read high because the hot coil would have a very strong magnetic field and would pull the pointer toward it. Technician B says the wire from the gauge to ground may be open. If this were the case, the gauge would never move away from cold because the hot coil would never be energized. **The correct answer is B.**

21. When performing a battery state of charge test with a hydrometer, you should subtract 0.004 specific gravity points from the hydrometer reading for every 10°F (5.6°C) of electrolyte temperature below 80°F (26.7°C). During this test, 0.004 specific gravity points must be added to the hydrometer reading for every 10°F (5.6° C) of electrolyte temperature above 80°F (26.7°C). The maximum variation is 0.050 in cell-specific gravity readings. When all the cell readings exceed 1.265, the battery is fully charged. **The only answer that is correct is A.**

22. Whenever you disconnect a battery, and for whatever reason, you should disconnect the negative cable first. Failure to do this can cause damage to the vehicle's components and you. Therefore Technician A is wrong and is thinking dangerously. Technician B is correct. Maintenance-free batteries with built-in hydrometers indicate a low charge (below 65 percent full charge) when the hydrometer is dark. The sight glass will appear green if the battery is over 65 percent charged. **Only B is the correct answer.**

23. Some two-speed wiper systems use a motor equipped with a shunt coil. The shunt coil is only energized during low-speed operation. Keep this in mind while looking through the possible answers to this question. Answer A links the shunt coil with high-speed operation. This is wrong. Answer C does the same thing and is also wrong. Answers B and D address different functions of the wiper system. Choice B deals with the park system. If the wipers park consistently in the same place, the park switch may be defective. So **answer B is the correct answer.** Answer D is just plain wrong. The wiper switch grounds the relay windings through the switch contacts. It does not ground the series field coils to turn on the wipers.

24. Both the wiper and the washer system do not work in this question. The problem must be somewhere in the shown circuit that is common to both systems. If you look carefully, there are only two points. Answer A has picked a potential problem that would affect only the washer circuit. Choices B and C both cite something that would affect the wiper system only but not the washers. Only D offers something that is common to both systems: an open ground. **D is the correct answer.**

25. This question uses the same diagram as question 24. It also uses the same sort of logic. In this case, the wipers work normally but the washer motor operates slowly. The cause of the problem must be located in that part of the circuit that controls the washer circuit. Technician A identified high resistance at a common ground as the cause. Tech A must have been thinking of the previous question. But that is not a likely cause this time. Technician B suspects high resistance in a wire to the washer motor. He is right. This could cause the problem. **The correct answer is B.**

26. The figure shows the hook-up for conducting a voltage drop test across the positive battery cable, from the battery to the battery terminal at the starter. The typical maximum allowable voltage drop across this cable is 0.1 volts. Therefore, **the correct answer is B.** Choice D has the right test and the right cable but has declared the voltage drop to be excessive when it is not. Answer A has two things wrong: the test is not measuring the negative cable and the voltage drop is not excessive. Choice C is wrong in the same way; it is the positive cable being measured and not the negative. How do you know that the cable is positive? The negative battery cable connects to the engine and/or chassis, not the starter. The cable being measured is connected to the starter.

27. An ohmmeter check is being taken across the solenoid S terminal and the solenoid case. The meter reads infinite which means there is no continuity between the two points. Answer A states the pull-in coil is shorted to ground. If it were, the reading would show very low resistance. Also, the ohmmeter leads must be connected across the solenoid terminal and the field coil terminal to test the pull-in winding. Choice B cites an open in the pull-in winding. An infinite reading certainly indicates an open. To test the pull-in winding, the ohmmeter leads should be connected from the solenoid terminal to the ground or solenoid case. **Answer B is correct.** Both choices C and D are wrong because they identify a short as a problem, just like A did.

28. The rheostat in the headlight switch determines the brightness of the instrument cluster bulbs. It is connected in series with the instrument cluster bulbs. Since it is in series, an open rheostat will open the circuit to the instrument cluster bulbs. Technician A is correct. Technician B, however, is wrong. The instrument cluster bulbs are connected in parallel to the battery. If one bulb burns out or opens, the other bulbs remain illuminated. **The correct answer is A.**

29. In an insulated side courtesy light system, the door jamb switches are connected between the battery positive terminal and the courtesy lightbulbs. In a ground-side system, the courtesy light circuit is completed when the door opens and the switch closes the circuit to ground. The system in this question is a ground-side system. In this case, both technicians are correct. A defective door jamb switch, causing a short to ground, would keep the lights on. So would a wire to a switch, if it had a short to ground. **The correct answer is C.**

30. This is an easy one, if you locate the circuit in the wiring diagram and understand what the diagram shows. The circuit that is shorted normally is the ground circuit for the under-hood lamp. When the hood opens, the switch provides a ground and the lamp lights. If the circuit has a short to ground, the switch will be bypassed and the light will be on continuously. **The correct answer is C.** The other circuits, suggested by the other answers, will not be affected by this short.

31. Technician A is correct. Some headlight door motors have a manual knob on the headlight door motors. If the motors do not open the doors, this knob may be rotated to lift the doors. Technician B is also correct, when the driver turns the headlights on, voltage is supplied from the battery through the headlight switch to Terminal A on the headlight door module. In response to this signal, the headlight door module supplies voltage to both headlight door motors. This action operates both motors to open the headlight doors. If the headlights are shut off, the module reverses the motor action to close the doors. **The correct answer is C.**

32. Following the wires in the diagram you will notice that the ground for the lights is redundant. Therefore if one is bad, the other will complete the circuit. For this reason, answer D is correct. Because the ground is redundant, all of the other individual sets of lights will work normally. **The correct answer is D.**

33. The hazard lights use basically the same circuit as the turn signals. The difference is in the control. Turn signals flash just at the side of the vehicle, and the hazard system flashes at all four corners. If there is a problem with the flashers and not with the turn signals as well, the problem can be in that part of the circuit that is only part of hazard light control. Of the answer choices given in this question, only B is unique to the hazards. Therefore, only it can be the cause of the problem. The other choices would affect turn signal operation, which work fine. **The correct answer is B.**

34. Many electronic instrument displays have self-diagnostic capabilities. In some electronic instrument displays, a specific gauge illumination or digital display will indicate defects in the display. Other electronic displays may be diagnosed with a scan tool. Technician A is correct. Other electronic instrument displays provide an initial indication of problems by displaying a code. This trouble code is designed to lead the technician toward a problem area. Technician B is also correct. **The correct answer is C.**

35. Thermal-electric gauges contain a bimetallic strip surrounded by a heating coil. The pivoted gauge pointer is connected to the bimetallic strip. The sending unit contains a variable resistor. In a fuel gauge, this variable resistor is connected to a float in the fuel tank. If the tank is filled with fuel, the sending unit resistance decreases, and the current flow through the bimetallic strip increases. This increased current flow heats the bimetallic strip and pushes the pointer toward the full position. If the fuel tank is full but reads less than full on the gauge, as is the case in this question, there must be some unwanted resistance in the circuit. Answer A describes a condition that matches that, high resistance in the ground circuit of the sending unit. Choice B cites low resistance in the sending unit. If this were the situation, the gauge would read higher than normal. The same is true for choice C. Answer D refers to an open in the circuit. If this were to happen, the gauge would not work at all. **A is the correct answer.**

36. To identify the cause of this problem, look at the wiring diagram and identify the part of the circuit that controls the indicator light. The problem is not in that part of the circuit. The defogger part of the circuit contains the problem. Answer A is not right. The indicator lamp would not illuminate if there were an open defogger relay winding. This would cause the defogger not to work, so it is half correct. The same is true for choice B. Choice C describes a condition that would prevent the defogger from working but would allow the indicator to light. Therefore, **C is the correct answer.** Answer D would prevent both the indicator and defogger from working.

37. Technician A says there should be no continuity between the antenna mast and the center pin on the lead-in wire. This is wrong. Continuity should be present between the end of the antenna mast and the center pin on the lead-in wire. Technician B also is wrong. Continuity should be present between the ground shell on the lead-in wire and the antenna mounting hardware. However, no continuity should exist between the center pin on the lead-in wire and the ground shell. **The correct answer is D.**

38. Technician A is correct. If a cruise control circuit loses the input from the VSS, the system will not work. Logic explains why. If the control module does not sense a speed, how can it set a speed? Technician B is not correct. If the gauge fuse is bad, the cruise control module will not be affected. The only thing that will happen is some of the gauges will not work. **The correct answer is A.**

39. Most common false alarms are caused by misplaced sensors or overly adjusted sensors, such as shock sensors. Most new shock and glass sensors now have two stage mechanisms where the sensor will give a warning when the first threshold is broken and will sound the alarm when the second threshold is broken. Door sensors will start to send false signals to the alarm module if they become rusted out or moving parts begin to wear out. Although the door, trunk, and hood ajar sensors should be checked, the first thing to check is the shock sensor. **Answer A is correct.**

40. Technician A is wrong. If the circuit was repaired correctly, there should be zero volts after the motor. Battery voltage should be dropped by the rest of the circuit. Also, Technician B is wrong. If everything was repaired correctly, the test light should illuminate with full brilliance at the power feed to the motor. That feed circuit before the motor will drop very little voltage. **D is the correct answer.**

41. Anytime there is a decrease in current flow, there is an increase in resistance. The only answer choice that cites this as the cause of the problem is B, and **B is the correct answer.** Low resistance will cause an increase in current. Therefore, choice A is wrong. With a short to ground comes high current, so choice C cannot be right. And choice D is wrong because there is no current flow when the circuit is open.

42. The meter shown for this question is measuring the voltage drop across the control circuit of a motor. Ideally there would be zero volts dropped. Because there is a large amount of voltage dropped across this part of the circuit, the motor would turn very slowly. Both technicians identified a possible source for this unwanted resistance. **The correct answer is C.**

43. With a normal total resistance in the circuit, the current should be 6 amps. We know this because of Ohm's law. The meter in this question reads 0.5 amps, which means the total resistance of the circuit increased by 22 ohms. That is a high resistance problem, just like Technician A says. Technician B correctly identifies a possible location for this resistance. Both technicians are correct and **the correct answer is C.**

44. Using jumper wires for diagnostics is an important technique. These, however, should only be used to bypass something. They are commonly used to bypass suspected opens and faulty switches, which is basically what Technician B said. But you should never do what Technician A said. Jumping across a fuse or component when the circuit has a short may damage the wiring harness of the vehicle or some other component. This is often called the "smoke test" and is certainly not recommended. **The correct answer is B.**

45. The device in the figure is a short detector. The needle responds to the magnetic field formed around a wire as current flows through it. The short detector is used in conjunction with a cycling circuit breaker connected into the circuit to replace the fuse. The needle of the detector will fluctuate as long as the gauge is over the conductor. The needle will stop fluctuating when the point of the short to ground is passed. Therefore, Technician A is correct. Since an open results in zero current flow, the detector cannot be used to find an open and Technician B is wrong. **The correct answer is A.**

46. To measure parasitic drain, a multimeter with a milliampere scale is connected in parallel to a current measuring block (tester) connected to the positive terminal of the battery. When the tester's switch is open, any current drain from the battery must flow through the meter. Some computers require several minutes after the ignition switch is turned off before they enter sleep mode with a reduced current drain. Therefore, after the ignition switch is turned off and the tester switch is opened, wait for the specified time before recording the milliampere reading. Some vehicle manufacturers specify a maximum battery drain of 50 milliamperes. A measured drain of 500 mA is too high. Technician A is correct in stating that the trunk light is staying on after the lid is closed. But the remaining drain is still too high. Technician B is also correct, there must be another drain. Both are correct and **the correct answer is C.**

47. When checking a fuse with a test light, the test light will illuminate when it is touched to both sides of the fuse. If the fuse is bad, the light will illuminate at only one side. In this case, the test light never comes on, so we know nothing about the fuse and Technician A is wrong. Technician B is correct in stating there is no power to the fuse since the test light did not illuminate at either side. **The correct answer is B.**

48. A battery's state of charge can be measured two ways: with a voltmeter and with a hydrometer. The voltmeter is connected across the battery and will measure at least 12.6 volts if the battery is fully charged. The hydrometer measures the specific gravity of the electrolyte. When all the cell readings exceed 1.265, the battery is fully charged. Both techs are right and **the correct answer is C.**

49. Batteries are either charged at a slow or fast rate. The charging time depends on the battery state of charge and the battery capacity. If the battery temperature exceeds 125°F (51.7°C) while charging, the battery may be damaged. When fast charging a battery, reduce the charging rate when specific gravity reaches 1.225 to avoid excessive battery gassing. The battery is fully charged when the specific gravity increases to 1.265. All of the answer choices in this question are correct, except C, which has no bearing on charging. However, if leakage was measured, clean the battery before charging it. **The correct answer is C.**

50. To properly jump-start a vehicle, begin by turning the accessories off in both vehicles. The negative booster cable must be connected to an engine ground in the vehicle being boosted. Always connect the positive booster cable first followed by the negative booster cable, and complete the negative cable connection last on the vehicle being boosted. Do not allow vehicles to contact each other. When disconnecting the booster cables, remove the negative booster cable first on the vehicle being boosted. The only answer choice in the question that is correct is D and **D is the correct answer.**

51. When a motor rotates at a slower speed than normal, it will draw more current than normal. Therefore, we have a basic explanation of what is happening to the starter in this question. Now the question is what is causing it. Technician A suggests that the starter has worn bushings. This is quite possible. If the armature cannot rotate freely, it will rotate slower and current will increase. Technician B states there may be high resistance in the battery ground cable. This would not cause a higher than normal current draw. Therefore, Technician B is not correct. **The correct answer is A.**

52. The measured voltage drop in this question is well beyond any specification and the problem needs to be fixed. All of the answer choices are possible locations for the problem, except choice C. High resistance in the starter field windings would not affect the measured voltage drop on the ground side of the starter, although it would affect starter operation. **The correct answer is C.**

53. When the starter does not work when activated, the cause of the problem can be no or little electrical power to the motor. A bad starter, solenoid, or internal engine problems may also cause this condition. Technician A is correct in stating that the problem could be caused by an open in the starter solenoid control circuit. Without this control, the starter and solenoid will not get power to operate. Technician B is also correct. A poor connection at the battery will cause an excessive voltage drop at that connection, leaving low voltage for the starter. Both technicians are correct and **the correct answer is C.**

54. The starter can make a high-pitched whining sound for two reasons and at two different times. If the clearance between the starter pinion gear and the flywheel is excessive, the starter will produce a high-pitched whine while the engine is being cranked. If the clearance is too small, the starter will make the high-pitched whine after the engine starts and the ignition switch is returned to the "run" position. This clearance is often controlled by shims at the starter to engine mounting point. Stating that the starter in this question needs to be reshimmed, Technician A is correct. Technician B is wrong in saying the clearance is excessive since the noise is evident after the engine starts and the ignition switch is returned to the "run" position. **The correct answer is A.**

55. The vehicle in this question has a slow crank and low current draw problem. Typically high starter current draw and low cranking speed usually indicates a defective starter. This condition may also be caused by internal engine problems, such as partially seized bearings. An engine that has low compression would behave nearly the opposite; it would crank fast but still draw low current. This is because the starter will rotate freer. Low current draw and slow cranking speed usually indicates excessive resistance in the starter circuit, just as Technician B suggests. **The correct answer is B.**

56. The only true way of ensuring that a drive belt is properly adjusted is using a belt tension gauge. So Technician B is correct. Distorting the belt or depressing it at a mid point are methods often used. These will give an idea of the condition and tension of the belt but are not the preferred way to check tension. Therefore, Technician A is not right. **The correct answer is B.**

57. The alternator belt tension and condition should be checked before an output test is performed. Turn off the vehicle accessories during the test. If the alternator is full-fielded during the output test, a carbon pile load in the volt ampere tester must be used to maintain the voltage below 15V. A typical charging system tester has battery leads and an inductive pickup lead that should be installed around the negative cables of the battery. The engine should be run at a fast idle (1500 to 2000 rpm), and adjust the carbon pile until the highest amperage is read. All of the answer choices is this question are true except B, and **B is the correct answer** of this "except" question.

58. When the alternator voltage is erratic or too low, the alternator may be full-fielded to determine the cause of the problem. When the alternator is full-fielded and the alternator current and voltage output are normal, the voltage regulator is probably defective. If the charging system voltage is higher than specified, the voltage regulator is probably defective. When the output is zero during the test, the field circuit is probably open. Worn brushes or an open field winding in the rotor usually causes this problem. If output is less than specified, there is probably a problem with the diodes or stator. A high resistance in the field winding also reduces output. When the alternator is full-fielded to test output, the voltage regulator is bypassed and does not affect output. Never full-field an alternator longer than 30 seconds. Both technicians are right and **the correct answer is C.**

59. Fusible links are circuit protection devices that are connected in series within a circuit. Technician A is correct in saying a good fusible link will have voltage at both ends of it. Technician B is also right. Fusible links should never be longer than nine inches. Links longer than this will decrease its protection ability. **The correct answer is C.**

60. Both technicians are correct. When replacing a composite or halogen bulb, always turn off the lights and allow the bulbs to cool before proceeding. Also, keep moisture away from the bulb, and handle the bulb only by its base. Do not scratch or drop the bulb. Coat the terminals of the bulb or at the connector with dielectric grease to minimize corrosion. Be careful not to get the grease on the bulb. **The correct answer is C.**

61. Some headlamp door retractors are vacuum operated. Any engine condition that would cause low vacuum will slow or prevent headlamp door operation. A jumped timing belt will affect engine vacuum and could affect the operation of the headlight doors. Technician A is right. The vacuum system is generally used to close the headlamp door, not keep it open as Technician B said. **The correct answer is A.**

62. This question is about one instrument panel light that does not work. The most obvious cause is a burned-out bulb, but neither technician guessed this. Rather, Technician A said the problem might be an open headlamp switch. If this were the case, all of the bulbs would not work. Technician B suspects an open ground for the printed circuit board. Again this problem would stop all of the bulbs from working. **The correct answer is D** because neither of the techs is right.

63. If the cigar lighter is pushed in and the cigar lighter fuse is blown, current flows through the dome light, courtesy light, and cigar lighter to the ground. Since these lights are now in series with the cigar lighter, the light glows dimly and the lighter cannot heat up properly. Therefore **answer B is correct.** Choices A and C would not prevent the cigar lighter from getting hot. Choice D has an open cigar lighter as the problem. If this were the case, the cigar lighter would not be hot because there would be no current flow available to it.

64. In many stoplight circuits, voltage is supplied to the brake light switch from the fuse box. When the brakes are applied, brake pedal movement closes the stoplight switch. This switch is typically mounted at the brake pedal assembly but may be installed in the master cylinder. The latter type switch is activated by the pressure buildup caused by the movement of the brake pedal. A very likely cause for all of the brake lights not working is the brake switch. Another likely cause is an open in power circuit. Both technicians gave a correct answer to this question and **the correct answer is C.**

65. Adding loads or resistors in parallel with a circuit will increase the circuit's current. When a tech adds lamps to an existing circuit, this could cause the fuse to blow. Technician A is right. Technician B is wrong because the additional current will not cause the signals to flash slower. They will tend to flash faster. **The correct answer is A.**

66. When bulbs are wired in series, all of the bulbs will go out when just one fails. In a parallel circuit, one bulb can go out and the others will work fine. Technician A is wrong. Since all of the lights do not work, Technician B could have identified the cause of the problem. An open in the power circuit will certainly stop the lamps from working. **The correct answer is B.**

67. Thermal-electric gauges contain a bimetallic strip surrounded by a heating coil. The pivoted gauge pointer is connected to the bimetallic strip. The sending unit contains a variable resistor. In a fuel gauge, this variable resistor is connected to a float in the fuel tank. If the tank is filled with fuel, the sending unit resistance decreases, and the current flow through the bimetallic strip increases. This increased current flow heats the bimetallic strip and pushes the pointer toward the full position. If the fuel gauge always reads empty, one can assume little or no voltage is available to the heating coil. All of the answer choices cite possible sources for this, except D. D is wrong. If a short were present in the circuit, current would be high and the gauge would always read full. **The correct answer is D.**

68. The IVR supplies about 5V to the gauges regardless of the charging system voltage. Technician A is wrong; a good IVR will not be affected by the charging system. Technician B is also wrong. Sending units should be tested with an ohmmeter. Bypassing them with a jumper wire may damage the gauge, whether or not there is an IVR in the circuit. Most sending units range from high to low resistance. Jumping across it would put zero resistance into the circuit and the gauge would receive high current. **The correct answer is D.**

69. Answer C relates to the external functioning of the turn signals. Since they work fine, this choice is wrong. Fiber-optic lighting is an integral part of a printed circuit board, so an open there would not prevent the indicator lamp from working. That means choice A is also wrong. Since the fiber-optic cable replaces a lightbulb, D cannot be right. The only possible answer is B. Therefore **the correct answer is B.**

70. Referring to the diagram for this question, you will see that Technician A is correct. An open winding in the horn relay would prevent the horn from working. If the winding were open, the relay would not close its contacts to send voltage to the horns. Technician B is wrong. A shorted horn switch would cause the horns to sound continuously. **The correct answer is A.**

71. **The correct answer is B.** Technician A incorrectly suggests that the wiper motor would cause the problem. If the motor were bad, the wipers would not work properly at all times and in other modes of operation. Technician B could be correct. Speed sensitive wipers rely on input from the VSS to regulate speed. If there is no speed input, there is nothing to set the wiper speed to.

72. Look at the answer choices carefully and think about the result of each problem. Then notice circuit V9 is a ground circuit. If that circuit is shorted to ground, who cares? It would just become a redundant ground. Now you know which of the answer choices is the least likely. **The correct answer is D.**

73. **The correct answer is C.** Both techs are correct. Looking at the Rd/Lt Gn wire near the motor, you will notice it is the power feed to the motor when the switch activates the "up" function. There should be 12 volts there, which is what Technician A said. Since that function of the system does not work, there may not be 12 volts there. You will also notice that the Yl/Lt Gn wire connects and completes the circuit from the circuit breaker at the motor to the up switch. If this circuit were open, the seat would not move up or down.

74. The defogger circuit is typical of many factory wiring diagrams. The basic wiring diagram is shown with all of the possible options as they may appear on different model vehicles. To answer the question and think about the problem the vehicle has, begin by looking at pin A of the defogger control. This is the terminal for the ground of the timer control. Since 7 volts is present here, we know there must be some resistance between that point and ground, which is what Technician B said. Technician A is wrong; there should be battery voltage (12 volts +) available to the grid. **The correct answer is B.**

75. Most power door locks rely on electric motors to lock and unlock the doors. Most of the motors are permanent magnet-type motors. Some power lock systems use solenoids to lock and unlock the doors. The center core of the solenoid is pulled into or pushed out of the solenoid's winding. This action is used on the lock mechanisms. Both technicians are correct. **The correct answer is C.**

76. To answer this question, you again need to locate the wires and components on the wiring diagram given with the question. Answer A suggests the problem is a shorted close switch. Since the problem is the inability of the roof to close, the short cannot cause the problem. The switch is designed to close the circuit by supplying a ground. If the ground were always there, the roof would not open. Choice B may be correct. An open in the close relay control circuit may stop the roof from closing. Choice C would shut down the whole system, as would choice D. **The correct answer is B.**

77. Use the diagram to gain an understanding of how this antenna circuit works. When the radio is turned on, voltage is supplied to the relay winding. This action moves the relay points to the up position, and current flows through the motor to move the antenna upward. When the antenna is fully extended, the up limit switch opens and stops the current flow through the motor. When the radio is turned off, current flow through the relay coil stops. Under this condition, the relay contacts move to the down position. This action reverses current flow through the motor and moves the antenna downward. When the antenna is fully retracted, the down limit switch opens and stops the current flow through the motor. Now apply what you know to what the two techs are saying. Technician A says the system uses a dual throw relay. That is correct. Only one set of contacts are closed at one time. Technician B says an open in the down limit switch would prevent the antenna from moving up. This cannot be correct. The down limit switch is normally open when the antenna is moving up. There would be change in the up operation. The antenna would not travel down. **The correct answer is A.**

78. Both technicians are correct. After a starter has been rebuilt or when a replacement starter is going to be installed, you should perform a free spin test before installing the starter into the vehicle. This allows you to make sure the motor works before you go through the trouble of installing it. Also, before mounting the starter, you should check the pinion to flywheel clearance. **The correct answer is C.**

79. Technician A is correct by saying that full fielding means the field windings are constantly energized with full battery voltage. This is done to measure the maximum output of a generator. Technician B, however, is wrong. Full fielding may be only necessary if the charging system did not pass its output test. **The correct answer is A.**

80. The condition in this question is one where the left rear and right rear taillights and the left rear brake light of a vehicle are dim whenever the brake pedal is depressed; however, the right rear brake light operates at the correct brightness. Technician A says the left rear taillight and brake light may have a poor ground connection. This is probably not correct as the right rear taillight also is dim. It is unlikely that the ground on the left side would affect both sides. However, some systems have a redundant ground for the rear lights. If that ground were bad, all of the rear lights would be dim. Technician B says the brake light switch may have excessive resistance. This is certainly wrong because it is not just the brake lights that are dim. Neither technician is correct. **The correct answer is D.**

81. The horn of a vehicle equipped with a horn relay sounds weak and distorted whenever it is activated. This problem can be caused by answer choices A, B, and C. It is very unlikely that the problem would be caused by D. Excessive voltage drop across the relay coil winding may not allow the horn to sound at all. If the resistance is too high, there may not be enough current flowing through the coil to energize the relay. **The correct answer is D.**

82. The circuit breaker that protects an electric window circuit blows whenever an attempt is made to lower the window. Whenever a circuit breaker blows, think of high current. Normally an increase in current is caused by a short. But higher than normal current draw by a motor can be caused by the motor's inability to rotate at its normal speed. Technician A is wrong. Excessive internal resistance in the motor would cause the current to decrease. Technician B is correct. If the window regulator is sticking, the motor would not be able to rotate at normal speed and current would be higher. **The correct answer is B.**

83. Slow engine cranking can be caused by over advanced ignition timing, misaligned starter mounting, and a low battery state of charge. All of the answer choices are true except B. A shorted neutral safety switch will allow the engine to start in any gear. **The correct answer is B.**

84. The noise cited in this question is caused by the free spin of the starter. Since the engine begins to crank at normal speed and then suddenly a "whee" noise is heard and the engine stops cranking, you know the starter is no longer cranking the engine. Technician A says the starter drive may be slipping and is probably right. Technician B says there may be excessive voltage drop across the starter solenoid contacts. This would cause the noise or the crank now, no-crank soon, problem. **The correct answer is A.**

85. The condition is that the starter will not crank the engine. A jumper wire is used to bypass the starter control circuit. When this is done, the starter is able to crank the engine. Technician A says this indicates the solenoid is bad. This is wrong. If the solenoid were bad, it would not work once the control circuit was bypassed. Technician B is right. A bad ignition switch would cause this problem, and it is being bypassed with the jumper wire. **The correct answer is B.**

86. The turn signals of a vehicle are inoperative and the indicator bulbs in the dash do not turn on when the turn signal switch is placed in either the right or left turn position. If the problem cited by Technician A were true, the turn signal bulbs would light but would not flash. Therefore Technician A is wrong. Technician B has identified a possible cause. If the circuit from the turn signal flasher to the turn signal switch were open, no power would be available to the circuit. **The correct answer is B.**

87. The basis of the question is that the low-speed mode of the wiper system shown in the figure does not work, but the high-speed mode does. To answer this question go to the circuit cited by the techs and think about what would happen if the circuit had the problem suggested by the techs. Technician A says circuit 58 may be open. If that circuit were open, no power would be available to the brush of the motor. This would cause the motor not to operate in low mode but would also cause the motor to operate at lower speeds when the high mode was selected. Therefore A is wrong. Technician B says circuit 63 may be open. This circuit carries battery current to the switch and washer assembly. If there were an open in this wire, nothing would work. **The correct answer is D.**

88. A voltmeter connected across the input and output terminals of an instrument cluster illumination lamp rheostat displays 12.6 volts with the switch in the maximum brightness position and the engine off. This means the voltage drop across the rheostat is 12.6 volts and the voltage available at the lamps will be 0.0 volts. Therefore, **the correct answer is B.** Answer A would be correct if the control were working properly, which it apparently is not. With a voltage drop of battery voltage across the rheostat, no voltage would be available to the lamps. Choice C states that the rheostat is working normally; this is wrong. Choice D is wrong because there is enough information to solve the problem.

89. Circuit 752 is the power feed from the switch to the resistor block. If this circuit were open, the medium-high speed mode would not work. It would also not affect the operation of the other modes. So Technician A is correct. Technician B says the middle resistor in the blower motor resistor assembly may be open. This resistor is part of the medium-low and low modes and is not part of the medium-high circuit. Therefore, an open in that circuit would not cause the problem. **The correct answer is A.**

90. The power window motor shown in the figure is completely inoperative. Different voltage measurements are given for terminals of the master window switch placed in the "down" position. To answer this question, go through each answer choice and check the validity by looking at the voltages given. Choice A suggests a faulty master switch. The switch is good because there are 12 volts at Terminal 3. The switch is completing the path for the down mode. Choice B states the window switch may be faulty. This also could not be right because there are 12 volts at Terminal 5. Answer C suggests that the motor is faulty. This is a probable cause of the problem. In fact, **the correct answer is C.** We know this because there are 12 volts applied to the motor and the ground circuit is complete. It has everything it needs to work. It just is not working. Choice D suggests a poor circuit ground. If this were the case, the motor would work in all modes but would be sluggish.

Glossary

Air bag A passive restraint system having an inflatable bag located in the center of the steering wheel in front of the driver and, in later model vehicles, a second inflatable bag located in the dash in front of the front seat passenger that inflates on vehicle impact.

Alternator A belt-driven generator that converts mechanical energy to electrical energy.

Antenna A wire or other conductive device used for radiating or receiving electromagnetic signals, such as those for radio, television, or radar.

Anti-theft system A deterrent system designed to scare off would be vehicle thieves.

Armature A part moved through a magnetic field to produce an electric current.

Backup light Lamps that provide rear illumination when the vehicle is being backed up.

Battery A device that converts chemical energy into electrical energy.

Bearing A component that reduces friction between a stationary and rotating part, such as a shaft.

Body control module A component of the computerized self diagnosis system.

Brake lights Red lamps at the rear of the vehicle that are illuminated when the brake pedal is applied.

Brake light switch A component of the braking system that completes an electrical circuit to illuminate the brake lights when the brake pedal is applied.

Brush An conductive component that rides on the commutator or slip ring to provide an electrical circuit between rotating and stationary components.

Bulb A glass envelope containing a filament to provide illumination.

Bulkhead connector A connector for wires that are to pass through the bulkhead of a vehicle.

Buzzer An electric sound generator that makes a buzzing noise.

Capacitor An electrical device for the temporary storage of electricity, often used to reduce RFI.

Charge The passing of an electric current through a battery to restore its energy.

Concealed headlights A headlamp system that retracts the lamps into the bodywork when they are turned off.

Corrosion A chemical action that eats away material such as metal, paint, or wire.

Courtesy light Lamps that illuminate the interior of a vehicle when a door is opened.

Cruise control A device that automatically maintains vehicle speed over a wide range of terrain conditions.

Current The flow of electricity, measured in amperes.

Current draw test A test to determine amperes required by the starter motor during starting operation.

Defogger A part of a heater system to prevent windshield or rear window fogging or icing.

Digital An electrical signal having two states, on and off.

Electric fuel pump An electrical device used to draw fuel from the fuel tank and deliver it to the engine.

Electronic ignition system An ignition system controlled by solid state electrical signals.

Field coil A coil of insulated wire, usually wound around an iron core, through which current is passed to produce a magnetic field.

Flywheel A heavy metal wheel that is attached to the crankshaft and rotates with it.

Fusible link A bar or wire that is designed to melt due to heat of a specific current passing through it is exceeded.

Ground The path, generally the body of the vehicle, for the return of an electrical circuit. Also, a term used for causing an accidental or intentional short circuit.

Harness A group of electrical conductors.

Hazard warning system Vehicle perimeter lighting and associated switches and wiring that flash giving warning to a hazard.

Headlamps The lamps at the front of a vehicle to provide illumination for the road ahead.

Horn relay An electromagnetic device used to activate the horn when the horn switch is closed.

Hydrometer An instrument used to measure the specific gravity of a liquid.

Ignition switch The main power switch, generally key operated, of a vehicle.

Inertia switch A switch found in the fuel pump circuit to turn off the fuel pump, and other vehicle accessories, in the event of a collision.

Interior lights Lighting in the interior of a vehicle, often called courtesy lights.

Linkage Levers or rods used to transmit power for one part to another.

Load A device connected to an electrical circuit to provide resistance and/or control the current flow.

Load test An electrical test for motors and batteries in which current draw and voltage is measured.

Module a control assembly designed to perform one or more specific tasks.

Ohm A unit of measure of electrical resistance.

Onboard computer The resident or main computer in a vehicle.

Open circuit An incomplete electrical circuit.

Power steering pump A hydraulic pump used to provide a fluid boost for ease in vehicle steering.

Printed circuit Electrically conductive circuit paths generally etched on a rigid or flexible strata.

Printed circuit board An insulated board on which a printed circuit is etched.

Schematic A drawing of a system using symbols to represent components.

Sending unit An electrical or mechanical sensing device to transmit certain conditions to a remote meter or gauge.

Series A part of an electrical circuit whereby one component is connected to another, as negative to positive, and so on.

Servo A device that converts hydraulic pressure to mechanical movement.

Short circuit The intentional or unintentional grounding of an electrical circuit.

Shunt A parallel electrical connection or circuit.

Speed sensor An electrical device that senses the speed of a rotating shaft or vibrating member.

Squeal A continuous high-pitched noise.

Starter The electric motor and drive used to start a vehicle engine.

Starter solenoid A magnetic switch used to engage the starter for starting an engine.

Switch A mechanical device used to open and close an electrical circuit.

Transmission A device used to couple a motor to a mechanical mechanism.

Troubleshoot To determine the problem, the cause of the problem, and the solution by systematic reasoning.

Turn signal Lights on the four corners of a vehicle to signal a turn.

Whine A continuous low pitch groaning or moaning-like sound.

Wiper A mechanical arm that moves back and forth over the windshield to remove water.

Notes

Notes